Herndon's Lincoln V2: The True Story Of A Great Life

William H. Herndon

2/09

Printing Statement:

Due to the very old age and scarcity of this book, many of the pages may be hard to read due to the blurring of the original text, possible missing pages, missing text, dark backgrounds and other issues beyond our control.

Because this is such an important and rare work, we believe it is best to reproduce this book regardless of its original condition.

Thank you for your understanding.

HERNDON'S LINCOLN

THE TRUE STORY OF A GREAT LIFE

Etiam in minimis major

THE HISTORY AND PERSONAL RECOLLECTIONS

OF

ABRAHAM LINCOLN

BY

WILLIAM H. HERNDON

FOR TWENTY YEARS HIS FRIEND AND LAW
PARTNER

AND

JESSE WILLIAM WEIK, A. M.

VOL. II

THE HERNDON'S LINCOLN PUBLISHING COMPANY

PUBLISHERS

SPRINGFIELD, ILLINOIS

CHAPTER IX.

THE year 1840 finds Mr. Lincoln entering his thirty-second year and still unmarried. "I have come to the conclusion," he suggests in a facetious letter, two years before, "never again to think of marrying." But meanwhile he had seen more of the world. The State Capital had been removed to Springfield, and he soon observed the power and influence one can exert with high family and social surroundings to draw upon. The sober truth is that Lincoln was inordinately ambitious. He had already succeeded in obtaining no inconsiderable political recognition, and numbered among his party friends men of wealth and reputation; but he himself was poor, besides lacking the graces and ease of bearing obtained through mingling in polite society—in fact, to use the expressive language of Mary Owens, he was "deficient in those little links which make up the chain of woman's happiness." Conscious, therefore, of his humble rank in the social scale, how natural that he should seek by marriage in an influential family to establish strong connections and at the same time foster his political fortunes! This may seem an audacious thing to insinuate, but on no other basis can we reconcile the strange course of his courtship and the tempestuous chapters in his married life. It is a curious history, and the facts, long chained down, are gradually coming to the surface. When all is at last known, the world I believe will divide its censure between Lincoln and his wife.

Mary Todd, who afterwards became the wife of Mr. Lincoln, was born in Lexington, Kentucky, December 13, 1818. "My mother," related Mrs. Lincoln to me in 1865, "died when I was still young. I was educated by Madame Mantelli, a lady who lived opposite Mr. Clay's, and who was an accomplished French scholar. Our conversation at school was carried on entirely in French—in fact we were allowed to speak nothing else. I finished my education at Mrs. Ward's Academy, an institution to which many people from the North sent their daughters. In 1837 I visited Springfield, Illinois, remaining three months. I returned to Kentucky, remaining till 1839, when I again set out for Illinois, which State finally became my home."

The paternal grandfather of Mary Todd, General Levi Todd, was born in 1756, was educated in Virginia, and studied law in the office of General Lewis of the State. He emigrated to Kentucky, was a lieutenant in the campaigns conducted by General George Rogers Clark against the Indians, and commanded a battalion in the battle of Blue Licks, August 18, 1782, where his brother, John Todd, was killed. He succeeded Daniel Boone in command of the militia, ranking as major-general, and was one of the first settlers in Lexington, Ky. February 25, 1779, he married Miss Jane Briggs. The seventh child of this union, born February 25, 1791, was Robert S. Todd, the father of Mrs. Lincoln. On her maternal side Mrs. Lincoln was highly connected. Her great-grandfather, General Andrew Porter, was in the war of the Revolution. He succeeded Peter Muhlenberg as major-general of the Pennsylvania militia. Her great uncles, George B. Porter, who was governor of Michigan, James Madison Porter, secretary of the navy under President Tyler, and David R. Porter, governor of Pennsylvania, were men of ability and distinction. Her mother, Anne Eliza Parker, was a cousin of her father, Robert S. Todd. The latter had served in both houses of the Kentucky Legislature, and for over twenty years was president of the Bank of Kentucky at Lexington. He died July 16, 1849.

To a young lady in whose veins coursed the blood that had come down from this long and distinguished ancestral line, who could even go back in the genealogical chart to the sixth century, Lincoln, the child of Nancy Hanks, whose descent was dimmed by the shadow of tradition, was finally united in marriage.

When Mary Todd came to her sister's house in Springfield in 1839, she was in her twenty-first year. She was a young woman of strong, passionate nature and quick temper, and had "left her home in Kentucky to avoid living under the same roof with a stepmother."* She came to live with her oldest sister, Elizabeth, who was the wife of Lin-

---

* Mrs. Edwards, statement, Aug. 3, 1887.

coln's colleague in the Legislature, Ninian W.
Edwards. She had two other sisters, Frances, married to Dr. William Wallace, and Anne, who afterwards became the wife of C. M. Smith, a prominent
and wealthy merchant. They all resided in Springfield. She was of the average height, weighing
when I first saw her about a hundred and thirty
pounds. She was rather compactly built, had a well
rounded face, rich dark-brown hair, and bluish-gray
eyes. In her bearing she was proud, but handsome
and vivacious. Her education had been in no wise
defective; she was a good conversationalist, using
with equal fluency the French and English lan-
guages. When she used a pen, its point was sure to
be sharp, and she wrote with wit and ability. She
not only had a quick intellect but an intuitive judgment of men and their motives. Ordinarily she
was affable and even charming in her manners; but
when offended or antagonized, her agreeable qualities instantly disappeared beneath a wave of sting-
ing satire or sarcastic bitterness, and her entire
better nature was submerged. In her figure and
physical proportions, in education, bearing, tempera-
ment, history—in everything she was the exact
reverse of Lincoln.

On her return to Springfield she immediately
entered society, and soon became one of the belles,
leading the young men of the town a merry dance.
She was a very shrewd observer, and discreetly and
without apparent effort kept back all the unattrac-
tive elements in her unfortunate organization. Her
trenchant wit, affability, and candor pleased the

young men not less than her culture and varied accomplishments impressed the older ones with whom she came in contact. The first time I met her was at a dance at the residence of Col. Robert Allen, a gentleman mentioned in the preceding chapter. I engaged her for a waltz, and as we glided through it I fancied I never before had danced with a young lady who moved with such grace and ease. A few moments later, as we were promenading through the hall, I thought to compliment her graceful dancing by telling her that while I was conscious of my own awkward movements, she seemed to glide through the waltz with the ease of a serpent. The strange comparison was as unfortunate as it was hideous. I saw it in an instant, but too late to recall it. She halted for a moment, drew back, and her eyes flashed as she retorted: "Mr. Herndon, comparison to a serpent is rather severe irony, especially to a newcomer."

Through the influence of Joshua F. Speed, who was a warm friend of the Edwardses, Lincoln was led to call on Miss Todd. He was charmed with her wit and beauty, no less than by her excellent social qualities and profound knowledge of the strong and weak points in individual character. One visit succeeded another. It was the old story. Lincoln had again fallen in love. "I have often happened in the room where they were sitting," relates Mrs. Edwards, describing this courtship, "and Mary invariably led the conversation. Mr. Lincoln would sit at her side and listen. He scarcely said a word,

but gazed on her as if irresistibly drawn towards
her by some superior and unseen power. He could
not maintain himself in a continued conversation
with a lady reared as Mary was. He was not educated and equipped mentally to make himself either
interesting or attractive to the ladies. He was a
good, honest, and sincere young man whose rugged,
manly qualities I admired; but to me he somehow
seemed ill-constituted by nature and education to
please such a woman as my sister. Mary was quick,
gay, and in the social world somewhat brilliant.
She loved show and power, and was the most ambitious woman I ever knew. She used to contend
when a girl, to her friends in Kentucky, that she
was destined to marry a President. I have heard
her say that myself, and after mingling in society in
Springfield she repeated the seemingly absurd and
idle boast. Although Mr. Lincoln seemed to be
attached to Mary, and fascinated by her wit and
sagacity, yet I soon began to doubt whether they
could always be so congenial. In a short time I
told Mary my impression that they were not suited,
or, as some persons who believe matches are made
in heaven would say, not intended for each other."

But Mrs. Edwards' advise was seed sown on
rocky soil. The courtship ran on smoothly to the
point of engagement, when a new and disturb-
ing element loomed up ahead in their paths. It
was no less than the dashing and handsome Stephen
A. Douglas, who now appeared on the scene in
the guise of a rival. As a society man Douglas
was infinitely more accomplished, more attractive

and influential than Lincoln, and that he should supplant the latter in the affections of the proud and aristocratic Miss Todd is not to be marveled at. He was unremitting in his attentions to the lady, promenaded the streets arm-in-arm with her— frequently passing Lincoln—and in every way made plain his intention to become the latter's rival. There are those who believe this warm reciprocation of young Douglas' affection was a mere flirtation on Mary Todd's part, intended to spur Lincoln up, to make him more de- monstrative, and manifest his love more positively and with greater fervor. But a lady relative who lived with Lincoln and his wife for two years after their marriage is authority for the statement coming from Mrs. Lincoln herself that "she loved Douglas, and but for her promise to marry Lincoln would have accepted him." The unfortunate attitude she felt bound to maintain between these two young men ended in a spell of sickness. Douglas, still hopeful, was warm in the race, but the lady's physician,—her brother-in-law,— Dr. William Wallace, to whom she confided the real cause of her illness, saw Douglas and induced him to end his pursuit,[*] which he did with great reluctance.

If Miss Todd intended by her flirtation with Douglas to test Lincoln's devotion, she committed a grievous error. If she believed, because he was ordinarily so undemonstrative, that he was without

---

[*] Mrs. Harriett Chapman, statement, Nov. 8, 1887.

will-power and incapable of being aroused, she certainly did not comprehend the man. Lincoln began now to feel the sting. Miss Todd's spur had certainly operated and with awakening effect. One evening Lincoln came into our store and called for his warm friend Speed. Together they walked back to the fireplace, where Lincoln, drawing from his pocket a letter, asked Speed to read it. "The letter," relates Speed, "was addressed to Mary Todd, and in it he made a plain statement of his feelings, telling her that he had thought the matter over calmly and with great deliberation, and now felt that he did not love her sufficiently to warrant her in marrying him. This letter he desired me to deliver. Upon my declining to do so he threatened to intrust it to some other person's hand. I reminded him that the moment he placed the letter in Miss Todd's hand, she would have the advantage over him. 'Words are forgotten,' I said, 'misunderstood, unnoticed in a private conversation, but once put your words in writing and they stand a living and eternal monument against you.' Thereupon I threw the unfortunate letter in the fire. 'Now,' I continued, 'if you have the courage of manhood, go see Mary yourself; tell her, if you do not love her, the facts, and that you will not marry her. Be careful not to say too much, and then leave at your earliest opportunity.' Thus admonished, he buttoned his coat, and with a rather determined look started out to perform the serious duty for which I had just given him explicit directions."

That night Speed did not go upstairs to bed with us, but under pretense of wanting to read, remained in the store below. He was waiting for Lincoln's return. Ten o'clock passed, and still the interview with Miss Todd had not ended. At length, shortly after eleven, he came stalking in. Speed was satisfied, from the length of Lincoln's stay, that his directions had not been followed.

"Well, old fellow, did you do as I told you and as you promised?" were Speed's first words.

"Yes, I did," responded Lincoln, thoughtfully, "and when I told Mary I did not love her, she burst into tears and almost springing from her chair and wringing her hands as if in agony, said something about the deceiver being himself deceived." Then he stopped.

"What else did you say?" inquired Speed, drawing the facts from him.

"To tell you the truth, Speed, it was too much for me. I found the tears trickling down my own cheeks. I caught her in my arms and kissed her."

"And that's how you broke the engagement," sneered Speed. "You not only acted the fool, but your conduct was tantamount to a renewal of the engagement, and in decency you cannot back down now."

"Well," drawled Lincoln, "if I am in again, so be it. It's done, and I shall abide by it."*

Convinced now that Miss Todd regarded the engagement ratified,—instead of broken, as her tall

---

* Statement, Joshua F. Speed, Sep. 17, 1866, MS.

suitor had at first intended.—Lincoln continued his
visits, and things moved on smoothly as before.
Douglas had dropped out of the race, and everything pointed to an early marriage. It was probably at this time that Mr. and Mrs. Edwards began
to doubt the wisdom of the marriage, and now and
then to intimate the same to the lady; but they
went no farther in their opposition and placed no
obstacle in their paths.

The time fixed for the marriage was the first day
in January, 1841. Careful preparations for the
happy occasion were made at the Edwards mansion.
The house underwent the customary renovation;
the furniture was properly arranged, the rooms
neatly decorated, the supper prepared, and the
guests invited. The latter assembled on the evening
in question, and awaited in expectant pleasure the
interesting ceremony of marriage. The bride, be-
decked in veil and silken gown, and nervously toy-
ing with the flowers in her hair, sat in the adjoining room. Nothing was lacking but the groom.
For some strange reason he had been delayed. An
hour passed, and the guests as well as the bride were
becoming restless. But they were all doomed to
disappointment. Another hour passed; messengers
were sent out over town, and each returning with
the same report, it became apparent that Lincoln,
the principal in this little drama, had purposely failed
to appear! The bride, in grief, disappeared to her
room; the wedding supper was left untouched; the
guests quietly and wonderingly withdrew; the lights
in the Edwards mansion were blown out, and dark-

ness settled over all for the night. What the feelings of a lady as sensitive, passionate, and proud as
Miss Todd were we can only imagine——no one can
ever describe them. By daybreak, after persistent
search, Lincoln's friends found him. Restless,
gloomy, miserable, desperate, he seemed an object
of pity. His friends, Speed among the number,
fearing a tragic termination, watched him closely in
their rooms day and night. "Knives and razors,
and every instrument that could be used for self-
destruction were removed from his reach."* Mrs.
Edwards did not hesitate to regard him as insane,
and of course her sister Mary shared in that view.
But the case was hardly so desperate. His condition
began to improve after a few weeks, and a letter
written to his partner Stuart, on the 23d of January,
1841, three weeks after the scene at Edwards' house,
reveals more perfectly how he felt. He says: "I
am now the most miserable man living. If what I
feel were equally distributed to the whole human
family, there would not be one cheerful face on
earth. Whether I shall ever be better, I cannot tell;
I awfully forebode I shall not. To remain as I am is
impossible. I must die or be better, as it appears
to me. . . I fear I shall be unable to attend to any
business here, and a change of scene might help me.
If I could be myself I would rather remain at home
with Judge Logan. I can write no more."

During all this time the Legislature to which Lincoln belonged was in special session, but for a time

---

* J. F. Speed, MS. letter, January 6, 1866.

he was unable to attend.* Towards the close
of the session, however, he resumed his seat. He
took little if any part in the proceedings, made no
speeches, and contented himself with answers to
the monotonous roll-call, and votes on a few of the
principal measures. After the adjournment of the
Legislature, his warm friend Speed, who had disposed of his interests in Springfield, induced Lincoln to accompany him to Kentucky. Speed's
parents lived in a magnificent place a few miles
from Louisville. Their farm was well stocked, and
they, in the current phrase, "lived well." Thither
he was taken, and there amid the quiet surroundings
he found the "change of scene" which he told
Stuart might help him. He was living under the
cloud of melancholia, and sent to the *Sangamon
Journal* a few lines under the gloomy title of "Suicide." They were published in the paper, and a
few years since I hunted over the files, and coming
across the number containing them, was astonished
to find that some one had cut them out. I have
always supposed it was done by Lincoln or by some
one at his instigation.

Speed's mother was much impressed with the
tall and swarthy stranger her son had brought
with him. She was a God-fearing mother, and besides aiding to lighten his spirits, gave him a Bible,

* His illness and consequent incapacity for duty in the Legislature, continued for almost three weeks. On the 19th of January, 1841, John J. Hardin announced his illness in the House.
Four days afterward he wrote the letter to Stuart from which
I have quoted a few lines.

advising him to read it and by adopting its precepts obtain a release from his troubles which no other agency, in her judgment, could bring him. "He was much depressed. At first he almost contemplated suicide. In the deepest of his depression he said one day he had done nothing to make any human being remember that he had lived; and that to connect his name with the events transpiring in his day and generation, and so impress himself upon them as to link his name with something that would redound to the interest of his fellow-men, was what he desired to live for."* The congenial associations at the Speed farm,† the freedom from unpleasant reminders, the company of his staunch friend, and above all the motherly care and delicate attentions of Mrs. Speed exerted a marked influence over Lincoln. He improved gradually, day by day gaining strength and confidence in himself, until at last the great cloud lifted and passed away. In the fall he and Speed returned to Springfield. At this point, as affording us the most reliable account of Mr. Lincoln's condition and views, it is proper to insert a portion of his correspondence with Mr. Speed. For some time Mr. Speed was reluctant to give these

---

* Letter, J. F. Speed, February 9, 1866, MS.

† At the time of Lincoln's visit at the Speed mansion, James Speed, a brother of Joshua, and afterward Attorney-General in Lincoln's Cabinet, was practicing law in Louisville. Lincoln came into his office daily. "He read my books," related Mr. Speed in after years; "talked with me about his life, his reading, his studies, his aspirations." Mr. Speed discredits the thought that Lincoln was insane at the time, although he understood he was saddened and melancholy over an unfortunate love affair.

letters to the world. After some argument, however, he at last shared my view that they were properly a matter of history, and sent them to me, accompanied by a letter, in which he says:

"I enclose you copies of all the letters of any interest from Mr. Lincoln to me. Some explanation may be needed that you may rightly understand their import. In the winter of 1840 and 1841, he was unhappy about his engagement to his wife— not being entirely satisfied that his heart was going with his hand. How much he suffered then on that account none knew so well as myself; he disclosed his whole heart to me.*

"In the summer of 1841 I became engaged to my wife. He was here on a visit when I courted her; and, strange to say, something of the same feeling which I regarded as so foolish in him took possession of me and kept me very unhappy from the time of my engagement until I was married. This will explain the deep interest he manifested in his letters on my account.

"One thing is plainly descernible; if I had not been married and happy—far more happy than I ever expected to be—he would not have married."

The first of these letters is one which he gave

---

* Lincoln wrote a letter—a long one which he read to me—to Dr. Drake of Cincinnati, descriptive of his case. Its date would oe in December, 1840, or early in January, 1841. I think that he must have informed Dr. Drake of his early love for Miss Rutledge, as there was a part of the letter which he would not read. . . I remember Dr. Drake's reply, which was, that he would not undertake to prescribe for him without a personal interview."—Joshua F. Speed, MS letter, November 30, 1866.

Speed when the latter started on his journey from Illinois to Kentucky. It bears no date, but was handed him January 1, 1842, as Speed has testified, in another letter to me, that he left Springfield on that day. It is full of consolation and advice how best to conduct himself when the periods of gloom which he feels sure will follow come upon his friend. "I know," he says, "what the painful point with you is at all times when you are unhappy; it is an apprehension that you do not love her as you should. What nonsense! How came you to court her? . . . Did you court her for her wealth? Why, you say she had none. But you say you reasoned yourself into it. What do you mean by that? Was it not that you found yourself unable to reason yourself out of it? Did you not think, and partly form the purpose, of courting her the first time you ever saw her or heard of her? What had reason to do with it at that early stage? There was nothing at that time for reason to work upon. Whether she was moral, amiable, sensible, or even of good character, you did not nor could then know, except perhaps you might infer the last from the company you found her in. . . . Say candidly, were not those heavenly black eyes the whole basis of all of your reasoning on the subject? After you and I had once been at the residence, did you not go and take me all the way to Lexington and back for no other purpose but to get to see her again on our return on that evening to take a trip for that express object?"

The next paragraph is significant as affording us

an idea of how the writer perhaps viewed Miss Todd's flirtation with Douglas: "What earthly consideration," he asks, "would you take to find her scouting and despising you and giving herself up to another? But of this you need have no apprehension, and therefore you cannot bring it home to your feelings."

February 3, he writes again, acknowledging receipt of a letter dated January 25. The object of Speed's affection had been ill, and her condition had greatly intensified his gloomy spirits. Lincoln proffers his sympathy. "I hope and believe," he continues, "that your present anxiety about her health and her life must and will forever banish those horrid doubts which I know you sometimes felt as to the truth of your affection for her. If they can once and forever be removed (and I almost feel a presentiment that the Almighty has sent your present affliction expressly for that object), surely nothing can come in their stead to fill their immeasurable measure of misery . . .

"It really appears to me that you yourself ought to rejoice and not sorrow at this indubitable evidence of your undying affection for her. Why, Speed, if you did not love her, although you might not wish her death, you would most certainly be resigned to it. Perhaps this point is no longer a question with you, and my pertinacious dwelling upon it is a rude intrusion upon your feelings. If so you must pardon me. You know the hell I have suffered on that point, and how tender I am upon it. You know I do not mean wrong. I have been quite clear of hypo since you left, even better than I was along in the fall."

The next letter, February 13, was written on the eve of Speed's marriage. After assurances of his desire to befriend him in everything, he suggests: "But you will always hereafter be on ground that I have never occupied, and consequently, if advice were needed, I might advise wrong. I do fondly hope, however, that you will never again need any comfort from abroad . . . I incline to think it probable that your nerves will occasionally fail you for awhile; but once you get them firmly graded now, that trouble is over forever. If you went through the ceremony calmly or even with sufficient composure not to excite alarm in any present, you are safe beyond question, and in two or three months, to say the most, will be the happiest of men."

Meanwhile Lincoln had been duly informed of Speed's marriage, and on the 25th he responds:

"Yours of the 16th, announcing that Miss Fanny and you are 'no more twain, but one flesh,' reached me this morning. I have no way of telling how much happiness I wish you both, though I believe you both can conceive it. I feel somewhat jealous of both of you now. You will be so exclusively concerned for one another that I shall be forgotten entirely. . . I shall be very lonesome without you. How miserably things seem to be arranged in this world! If we have no friends we have no pleasure, and if we have them we are sure to lose them, and be doubly pained by the loss."

In another letter, written the same day, he says, "I have no doubt it is the peculiar misfortune of both you and me to dream dreams of Elysium far exceeding all that anything earthly can realize. Far short of your dreams as you may be, no woman could do more to realize them than that same black-eyed Fanny. If you could but contemplate her through my imagination, it would appear ridiculous to you that any one should for a moment think of being unhappy with her. My old father used to have a saying, that, 'If you make a bad bargain hug it all the tighter,' and it occurs to me that if the bargain just closed can possibly be called a bad one it is certainly the most pleasant one for applying that maxim to which my fancy can by any effort picture."

Speed having now safely married, Lincoln's mind began to turn on things nearer home. His relations with Mary Todd were still strained, but reminders of his period of gloom the year before began now to bring her again into view. In a letter to Speed, March 27, he says:

"It cannot be told how it thrills me with joy to hear you say you are 'far happier than you ever expected to be.' That much, I know, is enough. I know you too well to suppose your expectations were not at least sometimes extravagant, and if the reality exceeds them all, I say, 'Enough, dear Lord.' I am not going beyond the truth when I tell you that the short space it took me to read your last letter gave me more pleasure than the total sum of all I have enjoyed since that fatal first of January, 1841. Since then it seems to me I should have been entirely happy but for the never-absent idea that there is one still unhappy whom I have contributed to make so. That kills my soul. I cannot but reproach myself for even wishing to be happy while she is otherwise. She accompanied a large party on the railroad cars to Jacksonville last Monday, and on her return spoke, so that I heard of it, of having enjoyed the trip exceedingly. God be praised for that!"

The last paragraph of this letter contains a bit of sentiment by Lincoln in acknowledgment of a violet. In the margin of the letter which he gave me, Speed made this note in pencil: "The violet was sent by my wife, who dropped it in the letter as I was in the act of sealing it. How beautiful the acknowledgment!" This is a paragraph: "The sweet violet you enclosed came safely to hand, but it was so dry, and mashed so flat, that it crumbled to dust at the first attempt to handle it. The juice that mashed out of it stained a place in the letter, which I mean to preserve and cherish for the sake of her who procured it to be sent. My renewed good wishes to her."

Meanwhile the coldness that existed between Lincoln and his "Mary" was gradually passing away, and with it went all of Lincoln's resolution never to renew the engagement. In a letter, July 4, he says; "I must gain confidence in my own ability to keep my resolves when they are made. In that ability I once prided myself as the only chief gem of my character; that gem I lost, how and where

you know too well. I have not regained it; and
until I do I cannot trust myself in any matter of
much importance. I believe now that had you
understood my case at the time as well as I understood yours afterwards, by the aid you would have
given me I should have sailed through clear; but
that does not now afford me sufficient confidence to
begin that or the like of that again . . . I always
was superstitious, I believe God made me one of
the instruments of bringing Fanny and you together, which union I have no doubt he had fore-
ordained. Whatever he designs he will do for me
yet. 'Stand still and see the salvation of the Lord,'
is my text just now. If, as you say, you have told
Fanny all, I should have no objection to her seeing
this letter, but for its reference to our friend here;
let her seeing it depend upon whether she has ever
known anything of my affairs; and if she has
not, do not let her. I do not think I can come to
Kentucky this season. I am so poor and make so
little headway in the world that I drop back in a
month of idleness as much as I gain in a year's
sowing."

The last letter, and the one which closes this
series, was written October 5, 1842. In it he simply
announces his "duel with Shields," and then goes
on to "narrate the particulars of the duelling business, which still rages in this city." This referred
to a challenge from the belligerent Shields to
William Butler, and another from General White-
sides to Dr. Merryman. In the latter, Lincoln
acted as the "friend of Merryman," but in neither

case was there any encounter, and both ended in smoke. The concluding paragraph of this letter is the most singular in the entire correspondence. I give it entire without further comment:

"But I began this letter not for what I have been writing, but to say something on that subject which you know to be of such infinite solicitude to me. The immense sufferings you endured from the first days of September till the middle of February you never tried to conceal from me, and I well understood. You have now been the husband of a lovely woman nearly eight months. That you are happier now than the day you married her, I well know, for without, you could not be living. But I have your word for it, too, and the returning elasticity of spirits which is manifested in your letters. But I want to ask a close question: 'Are you in *feeling* as well as *judgment* glad you are married as you are?' From anybody but me this would be an impudent question, not to be tolerated, but I know you will pardon it in me. Please answer it quickly, as I am impatient to know."

Lincoln again applied himself to the law. He re-entered the practice, after the long hiatus of rest, with renewed vigor. He permitted the memory of his engagement with Mary Todd to trouble him no longer. Their paths had diverged, the pain of the separation was over, and the whole thing was a history of the past. And so it might ever have remained but for the intervention of a very shrewd and sagacious lady—one who was capable of achieving success anywhere in the ranks of diplomacy. This lady was the wife of Simeon Francis, the editor of the *Sangamon Journal.* She was a warm friend of Mary Todd and a leader in society. Her husband was warmly attached to Lincoln. He ran the Whig organ, and entertained great admiration for Lincoln's brains and noble qualities. The esteem was mutual, and it is no stretch of the truth to say that for years Lincoln exercised undisputed control of the columns of the *Journal* himself. Whatever he wrote or had written, went into the editorial page without question. Mrs. Francis, sharing her husband's views of Lincoln's glorious possibilities, and desiring to do Mary Todd a kindly act, determined to bring about a reconciliation. She knew that Miss Todd had by letter a few days after "that fatal first of January, 1841," as Lincoln styled it, released him from the engagement, and that since then their relations had been strained, if not entirely broken off. As she viewed it, a marriage between a man as promising in the political world as Lincoln, and a woman as accomplished and brilliant in society as Mary Todd, would certainly add to the attractions of Springfield and reflect great credit on those who brought the union about. She was a great social entertainer, and one day arranged a gathering at her house for the express purpose of bringing these two people together. Both were invited and both attended; but neither suspected the other's presence. Having arranged things so ingeniously and with so much discretion, it was no difficult task for the hostess to bring the couple together by a warm introduction and the encouraging admonition, "Be friends again." Much to the surprise of both they found the web woven around them. They entered into the spirit of the reconciliation, and found Mrs. Francis' roof an inviting place for many succeeding meetings. A wall reared itself between them and the past, and they started again under the auspicious omens of another engagement. The tact of a woman and the diplomacy of society had accomplished what love had long since despaired of ever doing or seeing done.

The meetings in the parlor of Mrs. Francis' house were conducted with no little privacy. At first even Mrs. Edwards knew nothing of it, but presently it came to her ears. "I asked Mary," said this lady, "why she was so secretive about it. She said evasively that after all that had occurred, it was best to keep the courtship from all eyes and ears. Men and women and the whole world were uncertain and slippery, and if misfortune befell the engagement all knowledge of it would be hidden from the world."*

It is unnecessary to prolong the account of this strange and checkered courtship. The intervention of the affair with Shields, which will be detailed in a subsequent chapter, in no way impeded, if it did not hasten the marriage. One morning in November, Lincoln, hastening to the room of his friend James H. Matheney before the latter had arisen from bed, informed him that he was to be married

---

* Statement, January 10, 1866, MS.

that night, and requested him to attend as best
man.* That same morning Miss Todd called on her
friend Julia M. Jayne, who afterward married
Lyman Trumbull, and made a similar request. The
Edwardses were notified, and made such meager
preparations as were possible on so short notice.
License was obtained during the day, the minister,
Charles N. Dresser,† was sent for, and in the evening
of November 4, 1842, "as pale and trembling as if

---

* "Marriages in Springfield up to that time had been rather
commonplace affairs. Lincoln's was perhaps the first one ever
performed with all the requirements of the Episcopal ceremony.
A goodly number of friends had gathered, and while witnessing
the ceremony one of the most amusing incidents imaginable occurred. No description on paper can do it justice. Among those
present was Thomas C. Brown, one of the judges of the Supreme Court. He was in truth an "old-timer," and had the
virtue of saying just what he thought, without regard to place
or surroundings. He had been on the bench for many years and
was not less rough than quaint and curious. There was, of
course, a perfect hush in the room as the ceremony progressed.
Brown was standing just behind Lincoln. Old Parson Dresser,
in canonical robes, with much and impressive solemnity recited
the Episcopal service. He handed Lincoln the ring, who, placing it on the bride's finger, repeated the Church formula, 'With
this ring I thee endow with all my goods and chattels, lands and
tenements.' Brown, who had never witnessed such a proceeding, was struck with its utter absurdity. 'God Almighty! Lincoln,' he ejaculated, loud enough to be heard by all, 'the statute
fixes all that!' This unlooked-for interruption almost upset the
old parson; he had a keen sense of the ridiculous, and for the
moment it seemed as if he would break down; but presently recovering his gravity, he hastily pronounced them husband and
wife."—Letter, James H. Matheney, MS., Aug. 21, 1888.

† "My father, Rev. Charles Dresser, was a graduate of Brown
University, Providence, R. I., of the class of 1822."—Thomas
W. Dresser, MS. letter, Sept. 17, 1888.

being driven to slaughter," Abraham Lincoln was at last married to Mary Todd.*

One great trial of his life was now over, and another still greater one was yet to come. To me it has always seemed plain that Mr. Lincoln married Mary Todd to save his honor, and in doing that he sacrificed his domestic peace. He had searched himself subjectively, introspectively, thoroughly; he knew he did not love her, but he had promised to marry her! The hideous thought came up like a nightmare. As the "fatal first of January, 1841," neared, the clouds around him blackened the heavens and his life almost went out with the storm. But soon the skies cleared. Friends interposed their aid to avert a calamity, and at last he stood face to face with the great conflict between honor and domestic peace. He chose the former, and with it years of self-torture, sacrificial pangs, and the loss forever of a happy home.

With Miss Todd a different motive, but one equally as unfortunate, prompted her adherence to the union. To marry Lincoln meant not a life of luxury and ease, for Lincoln was not a man to accumulate wealth; but in him she saw position in society, prominence in the world, and the grandest social distinction. By that means her ambition would be satisfied. Until that fatal New Year's day in 1841 she may have loved him, but his action on

---

* While dressing for the wedding in his room at Butler's house, the latter's little boy, Speed, seeing Lincoln so handsomely attired, in boyish innocence asked him where he was going? "To hell, I suppose," was Lincoln's reply.

that occasion forfeited her affection. He had crushed her proud, womanly spirit. She felt degraded in the eyes of the world. Love fled at the approach of revenge. Some writer—it is Junius, I believe—has said that, "Injuries may be forgiven and forgotten, but insults admit of no compensation: they degrade the mind in its own self-esteem and force it to recover its level by revenge." Whether Mrs. Lincoln really was moved by the spirit of revenge or not she acted along the lines of human conduct. She led her husband a wild and merry dance. If, in time, she became soured at the world it was not without provocation, and if in later years she unchained the bitterness of a disappointed and outraged nature, it followed as logically as an effect does the cause.

I have told this sad story as I know and have learned it. In rehearsing the varied scenes of the drama,* I have unearthed a few facts that seem half

---

* For many years I had reason to believe that Sarah Rickard, who was a sister of Mrs. William Butler, had been the recipient of some attentions at the hand of Mr. Lincoln. The lady, long since married, is now living in a Western State. I applied to her for information recently, and after some entreaty received this answer in her own handwriting: "As an old friend I will answer the question propounded to me," though I can scarcely see what good it can do history. Mr. Lincoln did make a proposal of marriage to me in the summer, or perhaps later, in the year of 1840. He brought to my attention the accounts in the Bible of the patriarch Abraham's marriage to Sarah, and used that historical union as an argument in his own behalf. My reason for declining his proposal was the wide difference in our ages. I was then only sixteen, and had given the subject of matrimony but very little, if any, thought. I entertained the highest regard for Mr. Lincoln. He seemed almost like an older brother, being, as it were, one of my sister's family."

buried, perhaps, but they were not destined to lay buried deep or long. The world will have the truth as long as the name of Lincoln is remembered by mankind.

There were two things Mr. Lincoln always seemed willing to forget. One was his unparliamentary escape with Joseph Gillespie from the Legislature by jumping through the church window, in 1839, and the other was the difficulty with James Shields, or, as he expressed it in a letter to Speed, the "duel with Shields." Other incidents in his career he frequently called up in conversation with friends, but in after years he seldom if ever referred to the affair with Shields. People in Illinois did gradually forget or, at least, cease mention of it, but in more remote quarters where Mr. Lincoln was less extensively known, the thing, much to his regret, kept rising to the surface. During a visit which I made to the Eastern States in 1858, I was often asked for an account of the so-called duel; so often, in fact, that on my return home I told Mr. Lincoln of it. "If all the good things I have ever done," he said regretfully, "are remembered as long and well as my scrape with Shields, it is plain I shall not soon be forgotten."

James Shields, a "gallant, hot-headed bachelor from Tyrone county, Ireland," and a man of inordinate vanity, had been elected Auditor of State. Encouraged somewhat by the prominence the office gave him, he at once assumed a conspicuous position in the society of Springfield. He was extremely sensitive by nature, but exposed himself to

merciless ridicule by attempting to establish his
supremacy as a beau among the ladies. Blind to
his own defects, and very pronounced in support of
every act of the Democratic party, he made himself
the target for all the bitterness and ridicule of the
day. It happened that the financial resources of
the State, owing to the collapse of the great internal improvement system, were exceedingly limited,
and people were growing restless under what they
deemed excessive taxation. The State officers were
all Democrats, and during the summer they issued
an order declining to receive any more State Bank-
notes or bills in payment of taxes. This made the
tax-payer's burdens greater than ever, as much of
this paper remained outstanding in the hands of the
people. The order met with opposition from every
quarter—the Whigs of course losing no opportunity
to make it as odious as possible. It was perfectly
natural, therefore, that such an ardent Whig as
Lincoln should join in the popular denunciation.
Through the columns of the *Springfield Journal,* of
which he had the undisputed use, he determined to
encourage the opposition by the use of his pen.
No object seemed to merit more ridicule and caricature than the conspicuous figure of the Auditor of
State. At this time Lincoln was enjoying stolen
conferences under the hospitable roof of Mrs.
Francis with Mary Todd and her friend Julia M.
Jayne. These two young ladies, to whom he confided his purpose, encouraged it and offered to lend
their aid. Here he caught the idea of puncturing

Shields. The thing took shape in an article published in the *Journal*, purporting to have come from a poor widow, who with her pockets full of State Bank paper was still unable to obtain the coveted receipt for her taxes. It was written by Lincoln and was headed:

A letter from the Lost Townships.

Lost Townships, August 27, 1842.

Dear Mr. Printer,

I see you printed that long letter I sent you a spell ago. I'm quite encouraged by it, and can't keep from writing again. I think the printing of my letters will be a good. thing all around—it will give me the benefit . of being known by the world, and give the world the advantage of knowing what's going on in the Lost Townships, and give your paper respectability besides. So here comes another. Yesterday afternoon I hurried through cleaning up the dinner dishes and stepped over to neighbor S.... to see if his wife Peggy was as well as mout be expected, and hear what they called the baby. Well, when I got there and just turned round the corner of his log cabin, there he was, setting on the doorstep reading a newspaper. "How are you, Jeff?" says I. He sorter started when he heard me, for he hadn't seen me before. "Why," says he, "I'm mad as the devil, Aunt 'Becca!" "What about?" says I; "ain't its hair the right color? None of that nonsense, Jeff; there ain't an honester women in the Lost Townships than"— "Than who?" says he; "what the mischief are you about?" I began to see I was running the wrong trail, and so says I, "Oh! nothing: I guess I was mistaken a little, that's all. But what is it you're mad about?"

"Why," says he, "I've been tugging ever since

harvest, getting out wheat and hauling it to the river to raise State Bank paper enough to pay my tax this year and a little school debt I owe; and now, just as I've got it, here I open this infernal *Extra Register,* expecting to find it full of 'Glorious Democratic Victories' and 'High Comb'd Cocks,' when, lo and behold! I find a set of fellows, calling themselves officers of the State, have forbidden the tax collectors and school commissioners to receive State paper at all; and so here it is dead on my hands. I don't now believe all the plunder I've got will fetch ready cash enough to pay my taxes and that school debt."

I was a good deal thunderstruck myself; for that was the first I had heard of the proclamation, and my old man was pretty much in the same fix with Jeff. We both stood a moment staring at one another without knowing what to say. At last says I, "Mr. S—, let me look at that paper." He handed it to me, when I read the proclamation over.

"There now," says he, "did you ever see such a piece of impudence and imposition as that?" I saw Jeff was in a good tune for saying some ill-natured things, and so I tho't I would just argue a little on the contrary side, and make him rant a spell if I could. "Why," says I, looking as dignified and thoughtful as I could, "it seems pretty tough, to be sure, to have to raise silver where there's none to be raised; but then you see, 'there will be danger of loss' if it ain't done."

"Loss! damnation!" says he. "I defy Daniel Webster, I defy King Solomon, I defy the world— I defy—I defy—yes, I defy even you, Aunt 'Becca, to show how the people can lose anything by paying their taxes in State paper."

"Well," says I, "you see what the officers of State say about it, and they are a desarnin' set of men.

"But," says I, "I guess you're mistaken about what the proclamation says. It don't say the people will lose anything by the paper money being taken for taxes. It only says 'there will be danger of loss'; and though it is tolerable plain that the people can't lose by paying their taxes in something they can get easier than silver, instead of having to pay silver; and though it's just as plain that the State can't lose by taking State Bank paper, however low it may be, while she owes the bank more than the whole revenue, and can pay that paper over on her debt, dollar for dollar;—still there is danger of loss to the 'officers of State'; and you know, Jeff, we can't get along without officers of State."

"Damn officers of State!" says he; "that's what Whigs are always hurrahing for."

"Now, don't swear so, Jeff," says I; you know I belong to the meetin', and swearin' hurts my feelings."

"Beg pardon, Aunt 'Becca," says he; "but I do say it's enough to make Dr. Goddard swear, to have tax to pay in silver, for nothing only that Ford may get his two thousand a year, and Shields his twenty-four hundred a year, and Carpenter his sixteen hundred a year, and all without 'danger of loss' by taking it in State paper. Yes, yes: it's plain enough now what these officers of State mean by 'danger of loss.' Wash, I s'pose, actually lost fifteen hundred dollars out of the three thousand that two of these 'officers of State' let him steal from the treasury, by being compelled to take it in State paper. Wonder if we don't have a proclamation before long, commanding us to make up this loss to Wash in silver."

And so he went on till his breath run out, and he had to stop. I couldn't think of anything to say just then, and so I begun to look over the paper again. "Ay! here's another proclamation, or something like it."

"Another?" says Jeff; "and whose egg is it, pray?"

I looked to the bottom of it, and read aloud, "Your obedient servant, James Shields, Auditor."

"Aha!" says Jeff, "one of them same three fellows again. Well, read it, and let's hear what of it."

I read on till I came to where it says, "The object of this measure is to suspend the collection of the revenue for the current year."

"Now stop, now stop!" says he; "that's a lie a'ready, and I don't want to hear of it."

"Oh! may be not," says I.

"I say it—is—a—lie. Suspend the collection, indeed! Will the collectors, that have taken their oaths to make the collection, dare to suspend it? Is there anything in law requiring then to perjure themselves at the bidding of James Shields?

"Will the greedy gullet of the penitentiary be satisfied with swallowing him instead of all of them, if they should venture to obey him? And would he not discover some 'danger of loss,' and be off about the time it came to taking their places?

"And suppose the people attempt to suspend, by refusing to pay; what then? The collectors would just jerk up their horses and cows, and the like, and sell them to the highest bidder for silver in hand, without valuation or redemption. Why, Shields didn't believe that story himself: it was never meant for the truth. If it was true, why was it not writ till five days after the proclamation? Why didn't Carlin and Carpenter sign it as well as Shields? Answer me that, Aunt 'Becca. I say it's a lie, and not a well told one at that. It grins out like a copper dollar. Shields is a fool as well as a liar. With him truth is out of the question; and as for getting a good, bright, passable lie out of him, you might as well try to strike fire from a cake of tallow. I stick to it, it's all an infernal Whig lie!"

"A Whig lie! Highty tighty!"

"Yes, a Whig lie; and it's just like everything the cursed British Whigs do. First they'll do some divilment, and then they'll tell a lie to hide it. And they don't care how plain a lie it is: they think they can cram any sort of a one down the throats of the ignorant Locofocos, as they call the Democrats."

"Why, Jeff, you're crazy: you don't mean to say Shields is a Whig!"

"Yes, I do."

"Why, look here! the proclamation is in your own Democratic paper, as you call it."

"I know it; and what of that? They only printed it to let us Democrats see the deviltry the Whigs are at."

"Well, but Shields is the auditor of this Loco— I mean this Democratic State."

"So he is, and Tyler appointed him to office."

"Tyler appointed him?"

"Yes (if you must chaw it over), Tyler appointed him; or, if it wasn't him, it was old Granny Harrison, and that's all one. I tell you, Aunt 'Becca, there's no mistake about his being a Whig. Why, his very looks shows it; everything about him shows it: if I was deaf and blind, I could tell him by the smell. I seed him when I was down in Springfield last winter. They had a sort of a gatherin' there one night among the grandees, they called a fair. All the gals about town was there, and all the handsome widows and married women, finickin' about trying to look like gals, tied as tight in the middle, and puffed out at both ends, like bundles of fodder that hadn't been stacked yet, but wanted stackin' pretty

bad. And then they had tables all around the
house kivered over with [   ] caps and pincush-
ions and ten thousands such little knic-knacks, tryin'
to sell 'em to the fellows that were bowin' and
scrapin' and kungeerin' about 'em.   They wouldn't
let no Democrats in, for fear they'd disgust the
ladies, or scare the little gals, or dirty the floor.   I
looked in at the window, and there was this same
fellow Shields floatin' about on the air, without heft
or earthly substances, just like a lock of cat fur
where cats had been fighting.

"He was paying his money to this one, and that
one, and t'other one, and sufferin' great loss because
it wasn't silver instead of State paper; and the
sweet distress he seemed to be in,—his very features, in the ecstatic agony of his soul, spoke audibly
and distinctly, 'Dear girls, it is distressing, but I
cannot marry you all.   Too well I know how much
you suffer; but do, do remember, it is not my fault
that I am so handsome and so interesting.'

"As this last was expressed by a most exquisite
contortion of his face, he seized hold of one of their
hands, and squeezed, and held on to it about a quarter of an hour.   'Oh, my good fellow!' says I to
myself, 'if that was one of our Democratic gals in
the Lost Townships, the way you'd get a brass pin
let into you would be about up to the head.'   He
a Democrat! Fiddlesticks! I tell you, Aunt 'Becca,
he's a Whig, and no mistake: nobody but a Whig
could make such a conceity dunce of himself."

"Well," says I, "maybe he is; but, if he is, I'm
mistaken the worst sort.   Maybe so, maybe so;
but, if I am, I'll suffer by it; I'll be a Democrat if
it turns out that Shields is a Whig, considerin' you
shall be a Whig if he turns out a Democrat."

"A bargain, by jingoes!" says he; "but how
will we find out?"

"Why," says I, "we'll just write and ax the printer."

"Agreed again!" says he; "and by thunder! if
it does turn out that Shields is a Democrat, I never
will"—

"Jefferson! Jefferson!"

"What do you want, Peggy?"

"Do get through your everlasting clatter some
time, and bring me a gourd of water; the child's
been crying for a drink this livelong hour."

"Let it die, then; it may as well die for water as
to be taxed to death to fatten officers of State."

Jeff run off to get the water, though, just like he
hadn't been saying anything spiteful for he's a
raal good-hearted fellow, after all, once you get at
the foundation of him.

I walked into the house, and, "Why, Peggy," says
I, "declare we like to forgot you altogether."

"Oh, yes," says she, "when a body can't help
themselves, everybody soon forgets 'em; but, thank
God! by day after to-morrow I shall be well
enough to milk the cows, and pen the calves, and
wring the contrary ones' tails for 'em, and no
thanks to nobody."

"Good evening, Peggy," says I, and so I sloped,
for I seed she was mad at me for making Jeff neglect her so long.

And now, Mr. Printer, will you be sure to let us
know in your next paper whether this Shields is a
Whig or a Democrat? I don't care about it for my
self, for I know well enough how it is already; but
I want to convince Jeff. It may do some good to let
him, and others like him, know who and what these
officers of State are. It may help to send the present hypocritical set to where they belong, and to fill
the places they now disgrace, with men who will do
more work for less pay, and take a fewer airs while
they are doing it. It ain't sensible to think that the

same men who get us into trouble will change their
course; and yet it's pretty plain if some change for
the better is not made, it's not long that either
Peggy or I or any of us will have a cow left to
milk, or calf's tail to wring.

Yours truly,

REBECCA ———.

Within a week another epistle from Aunt Rebecca appeared, in which, among other things, she
offered the gallant Shields her hand. This one
was written by Miss Todd and Miss Jayne. I
insert it without further comment:

LOST TOWNSHIPS, September 8, 1842.

DEAR MR. PRINTER:

I was a-standin' at the spring yesterday a-wash-
in' out butter when I seed Jim Snooks a-ridin' up
towards the house for very life, when, jist as I was
a-wonderin' what on airth was the matter with him,
he stops suddenly, and ses he, "Aunt 'Becca, here's
somethin' for you;" and with that he hands out
your letter. Well, you see, I steps out towards
him, not thinkin' that I had both hands full of butter; and seein' I couldn't take the letter, you know,
without greasin' it, I ses, "Jim, jist you open it, and
read it for me." Well, Jim opens it and reads it;
and would you believe it, Mr. Editor, I was so completely dumfounded and turned into stone that
there I stood in the sun a-workin' the butter, and
it a-running on the ground, while he read the letter,
that I never thunk what I was about till the hull
on't run melted on the ground and was lost. Now,
sir, it's not for the butter, nor the price of the butter, but, the Lord have massy on us, I wouldn't
have sich another fright for a whole firkin of it.
Why, when I found out that it was the man what
Jeff seed down to the fair that had demanded the

author of my letters, threatnin' to take personal satisfaction of the writer, I was so skart that I tho't I should quill-wheel right where I was.

You say that Mr. S—— is offended at being compared to cats' fur, and is as mad as a March hare (that ain't fur), because I told about the squeezin'. Now I want you to tell Mr. S——that, rather than fight, I'll make any apology; and, if he wants personal satisfaction, let him only come here, and he may squeeze my hand as hard as I squeezed the butter, and, if that ain't personal satisfaction, I can only say that he is the fust man that was not satisfied with squeezin' my hand. If this should not answer, there is one thing more that I would rather do than get a lickin'. I have long expected to die a widow; but, as Mr. S—— is rather good-looking than otherwise, I must say I don't care if we compromise the matter by—really, Mr. Printer, I can't help blushin'—but I—it must come out—I—but widowed modesty—well, if I must, I must—wouldn't he—may be sorter let the old grudge drap if I was to consent to be—be—h-i-s w-i-f-e? I know he's a fightin' man, and would rather fight than eat; but isn't marryin' better than fightin', though it does sometimes run in to it? And I don't think, upon the whole, that I'd be sich a bad match neither: I'm not over sixty, and am jist four feet three in my bare feet, and not much more around the girth; and for color, I wouldn't turn my back to nary a gal in the Lost Townships. But, after all, maybe I'm countin' my chickins before they are hatched, and dreamin' of matrimonial bliss when the only alternative reserved for me may be a lickin'. Jeff tells me the way these fire-eaters do is to give the challenged party choice of weapons, etc., which bein' the case, I'll tell you in confidence that I never fights with anything but broomsticks or hot water or a shovelful of coals or some such thing;

the former of which, being somewhat like a shilla-
lah, may not be very objectional to him. I will give
him choice, however, in one thing, and that is,
whether, when we fight, I shall wear breeches or
he petticoats, for, I presume that change is sufficient to place us on an equality.

　　　　　　　　　　Yours, etc.,

　　　　　　　　　　　　Rebecca———.

P. S.—Jist say to your friend, if he concludes to
marry rather than fight, I shall only inforce one
condition, that is, if he should ever happen to
gallant any young gals home of nights from our
house, he must not squeeze their hands.

Not contented with their epistolary efforts, the
ladies invoked the muse. "Rebecca" deftly trans-
formed herself into "Cathleen," and in jingling
ryhme sang the praises of Shields, and congratulated
him over the prospect of an early marriage to the
widow. Following are the verses, rhyme, metre,
and all:

> Ye Jew's harps awake! The Auditor's won.
> Rebecca the widow has gained Erin's son;
> The pride of the north from Emerald Isle
> Has been wooed and won by a woman's smile.
> The combat's relinquished, old loves all forgot:
> To the widow he's bound. Oh, bright be his lot!
> In the smiles of the conquest so lately achieved.
> Joyful be his bride, "widowed modesty" relieved.
> The footsteps of time tread lightly on flowers,
> May the cares of this world ne'er darken his hours!
> But the pleasures of life are fickle and coy
> As the smiles of a maiden sent off to destroy.
> Happy groom! In sadness far distant from thee
> The fair girls dream only of past times of glee

Enjoyed in thy presence; whilst the soft blarnied store
Will be fondly remembered as relics of yore,
And hands that in rapture you oft would have pressed,
In prayer will be clasped that your lot may be blest.

CATHLEEN.

The satire running through these various compositions, and the publicity their appearance in the *Journal* gave them, had a most wonderful effect on the vain and irascible Auditor of State. He could no longer endure the merriment and ridicule that met him from every side. A man of cooler head might have managed it differently, but in the case of a high-tempered man like Shields he felt that his integrity had been assailed and that nothing but an "affair of honor" would satisfy him. Through General John D. Whiteside he demanded of editor Francis the name of the author. The latter hunted up Lincoln, who directed him to give his name and say nothing about the ladies. The further proceedings in this grotesque drama were so graphically detailed by the friends of both parties in the columns of the *Journal* at that time, that I copy their letters as a better and more faithful narrative than can be obtained from any other source. The letter of Shields' second, General Whiteside, appearing first in the *Journal*, finds the same place in this chapter:

"SPRINGFIELD, Oct. 3, 1842.
"To the Editor of the Sangamon Journal:
"SIRS: To prevent misrepresentation of the recent affair between Messrs. Shields and Lincoln, I think it proper to give a brief narrative of the

facts of the case, as they came within my knowledge; for the truth of which I hold myself responsible, and request you to give the same publication. An offensive article in relation to Mr.
Shields appeared in the *Sangamon Journal* of the
2d of September last; and, on demanding the
author, Mr. Lincoln was given up by the editor.
Mr. Shields, previous to this demand, made
arrangements to go to Quincy on public business;
and before his return Mr. Lincoln had left for
Tremont to attend the court, with the intention,
as we learned, of remaining on the circuit several
weeks. Mr. Shields, on his return, requested me to
accompany him to Tremont; and, on arriving
there, we found that Dr. Merryman and Mr. Butler
had passed us in the night, and got there before us.
We arrived in Tremont on the 17th ult., and Mr.
Shields addressed a note to Mr. Lincoln immediately, informing him that he was given up as the
author of some articles that appeared in the *Sangamon Journal* (one more over the signature having
made its appearance at this time), and requesting
him to retract the offensive allusions contained in
said articles in relation to his private character.
Mr. Shields handed this note to me to deliver to
Mr. Lincoln, and directed me, at the same time,
not to enter into any verbal communication, or be
the bearer of any verbal explanation, as such were
always liable to misapprehension. This note was
delivered by me to Mr. Lincoln, stating, at the
same time, that I would call at his convenience for
an answer. Mr. Lincoln, in the evening of the
same day, handed me a letter addressed to Mr.
Shields. In this he gave or offered no explanation,
but stated therein that he could not submit to
answer further, on the ground that Mr. Shield's
note contained an assumption of facts and also a
menace. Mr. Shields then addressed him another

note, in which he disavowed all intention to menace, and requested to know whether he (Mr. Lincoln) was author of either of the articles which appeared in the *Journal*, headed 'Lost Townships,' and signed 'Rebecca'; and, if so, he repeated his request of a retraction of the offensive matter in relation to his private character; if not, his denial would be held sufficient. This letter was returned to Mr. Shields unanswered, with a verbal statement 'that there could be no further negotiation between them until the first note was withdrawn.' Mr. Shields thereupon sent a note designating me as a friend, to which Mr. Lincoln relied by designating Dr. Merryman. These three last notes passed on Monday morning, the 19th. Dr. Merryman handed me Mr. Lincoln's last note when by ourselves. I remarked to Dr. Merryman that the matter was not submitted to us, and that I would propose that he and myself should pledge our words of honor to each other to try to agree upon terms of amicable arrangement, and compel our principals to accept of them. To this he readily assented, and we shook hands upon the pledge. It was then mutually agreed that we should adjourn to Springfield, and there procrastinate the matter, for the purpose of effecting the secret arrangement between him and myself. All this I kept concealed from Mr. Shields. Our horse had got a little lame in going to Tremont, and Dr. Merryman invited me to take a seat in his buggy. I accepted the invitation the more readily, as I thought that leaving Mr. Shields in Tremont until his horse would be in better condition to travel would facilitate the private agreement between Dr. Merryman and myself. I travelled to Springfield part of the way with him, and part with Mr. Lincoln; but nothing passed between us on the journey in relation to the matter in hand. We arrived in Springfield on Monday

night. About noon on Tuesday, to my astonishment, a proposition was made to meet in Missouri,
within three miles of Alton, on the next Thursday!
The weapons, cavalry broadswords of the largest
size; the parties to stand on each side of a barrier,
and to be confined to a limited space. As I had
not been consulted at all on the subject, and considering the private understanding between Dr.
Merryman and myself, and it being known that Mr.
Shields was left at Tremont, such a proposition
took me by surprise. However, being determined
not to violate the laws of the State, I declined
agreeing upon the terms until we should meet in
Missouri. Immediately after, I called upon Dr.
Merryman and withdrew the pledge of honor between him and myself in relation to a secret arrangement. I started after this to meet Mr. Shields, and
met him about twenty miles from Springfield. It
was late on Tuesday night when we both reached the
city and learned that Dr. Merryman had left for
Missouri, Mr. Lincoln having left before the proposition was made, as Dr. Merryman had himself
informed me. The time and place made it necessary to start at once. We left Springfield at eleven
o'clock on Tuesday night, travelled all night, and
arrived in Hillsborough on Wednesday morning,
where we took in General Ewing. From there we
went to Alton, where we arrived on Thursday; and,
as the proposition required three friends on each
side, I was joined by General Ewing and Dr. Hope,
as the friends of Mr. Shields. We then crossed to
Missouri, where a proposition was made by General
Hardin and Dr. English (who had arrived there in
the mean time as mutual friends) to refer the
matter to, I think, four friends for a settlement.
This I believed Mr. Shields would refuse, and declined seeing him; but Dr. Hope, who conferred
with him upon the subject, returned and stated that

Mr. Shields declined settling the matter through any other than the friends he had selected to stand by him on that occasion. The friends of both the parties finally agreed to withdraw the papers (temporarily) to give the friends of Mr. Lincoln an opportunity to explain. Whereupon the friends of Mr. Lincoln, to wit, Messrs. Merryman, Bledsoe, and Butler, made a full and satisfactory explanation in relation to the article which appeared in the *Sangamon Journal* of the 2d, the only one written by him. This was all done without the knowledge or consent of Mr. Shields, and he refused to accede to it, until Dr. Hope, General Ewing, and myself declared the apology sufficient, and that we could not sustain him in going further. I think it necessary to state further, that no explanation or apology had been previously offered on the part of Mr. Lincoln to Mr. Shields, and that none was ever communicated by me to him, nor was any even offered to me, unless a paper read to me by Dr. Merryman after he had handed me the broadsword proposition on Tuesday. I heard so little of the reading of the paper, that I do not know fully what it purported to be; and I was the less inclined to inquire, as Mr. Lincoln was then gone to Missouri, and Mr. Shields not yet arrived from Tremont. In fact, I could not entertain any offer of the kind, unless upon my own responsibility; and that I was not disposed to do after what had already transpired.

"I make this statement, as I am about to be absent for some time, and I think it due to all concerned to give a true version of the matter before I leave.

"Your obedient servant,

"JOHN D. WHITESIDE."

SPRINGFIELD, October 8, 1842.

Editors of the Journal:

GENTS:—By your paper of Friday, I discover that General Whiteside has published his version of the late affair between Messrs. Shields and Lincoln, I now bespeak a hearing of my version of the same affair, which shall be true and full as to all material facts.

On Friday evening, the 16th of September, I learned that Mr. Shields and General Whiteside had started in pursuit of Mr. Lincoln, who was at Tremont, attending court. I knew that Mr. Lincoln was wholly unpractised both as to the diplomacy and weapons commonly employed in similar affairs; and I felt it my duty, as a friend, to be with him, and, so far as in my power, to prevent any advantage being taken of him as to either his honor or his life. Accordingly, Mr. Butler and myself started, passed Shields and Whiteside in the night, and arrived at Tremont ahead of them on Saturday morning. I told Mr. Lincoln what was brewing, and asked him what course he proposed to himself. He stated that he was wholy opposed to duelling, and would do anything to avoid it that might not degrade him in the estimation of himself and friends; but, if such degradation or a fight were the only alternatives, he would fight.

In the afternoon Shields and Whiteside arrived, and very soon the former sent to Mr. Lincoln, by the latter, the following note or letter:—

TREMONT, September 17, 1842.

A. LINCOLN, Esq. :—I regret that my absence on public business compelled me to postpone a matter of private consideration a little longer than I could have desired. It will only be necessary, however, to account for it by informing you that I have been to Quincy on business that would not admit of delay. I will now state briefly the reasons of my troubling you with this communication, the disagreeable nature of which I regret, as I had hoped to avoid any difficulty with any one in Springfield while residing there, by endeavoring to conduct myself in such a way amongst both my political friends and opponents, as to escape the necessity of any. Whilst thus abstaining from giving provocation, I have become the object of slander, vituperation, and personal abuse which, were I capable of submitting to, I would prove myself worthy of the whole of it.

In two or three of the last numbers of the *Sangamon Journal*, articles of the most personal nature, and calculated to degrade me, have made their appearance. On inquiring, I was informed by the editor of that paper, through the medium of my friend, General Whiteside, that you are the author of those articles. This information satisfies me that I have become, by some means or other, the object of secret hostility. I will not take the trouble of inquiring into the reason of all this, but I will take the liberty of requiring a full, positive, and absolute retraction of all offensive allusions used by you in these communications, in relation to my private character and standing as a man, as an apology for the insults conveyed in them.

This may prevent consequences which no one will regret more than myself.

Your ob't serv't,

Jas. Shields.

About sunset, General Whiteside called again, and secured from Mr. Lincoln the following answer to Mr. Shield's note:—

Tremont, September 17, 1842.

Jas. Shields, Esq. :—Your note of to-day was handed me by General Whiteside. In that note you say you have been informed, through the medium of the editor of the *Journal*, that I am the author of certain articles in that paper which you deem personally abusive of you; and, without stopping to inquire whether I really am the author, or to point out what is offensive in them, you demand an unqualified retraction of all that is offensive, and then proceed to hint at consequences.

Now, sir, there is in this so much assumption of facts, and so much of menace as to consequences, that I cannot submit to answer that note any further than I have, and to add, that the consequences to which I suppose you allude would be matter of as great regret to me as it possibly could to you.

Respectfully,

A. LINCOLN.

In about an hour, General Whiteside called again with another note from Mr. Shields; but after conferring with Mr. Butler for a long time, say two or three hours, returned without presenting the note to Mr. Lincoln. This was in consequence of an assurance from Mr. Butler that Mr. Lincoln could not receive any communication from Mr. Shields, unless it were a withdrawal of his first note, or a challenge. Mr. Butler further stated to General Whiteside, that, on the withdrawal of the first note, and a proper and gentlemanly request for an explanation, he had no doubt one would be given. General Whiteside admitted that that was the course Mr. Shields ought to pursue, but deplored that his furious and intractable temper prevented his having any influence with him to that end. General Whiteside then requested us to wait with him until Monday morning, that he might endeavor to bring Mr. Shields to reason.

On Monday morning he called and presented Mr. Lincoln the same note as Mr. Butler says he had brought on Saturday evening. It was as follows:—

TREMONT, September 17, 1842.

A. LINCOLN, Esq. :—In your reply to my note of this date, you intimate that I assume facts and menace consequences, and that you cannot submit to answer it further. As now, sir, you desire it, I will be a little more particular. The editor of the *Sangamon Journal* gave me to understand that you are the author of an article which appeared, I think, in that paper of the 2d September inst., headed "The Lost Townships" and signed Rebecca or 'Becca. I would therefore take the liberty of asking whether you are the author of said article, or any other of the same signature which has appeared in any of the late numbers of that paper. If so, I repeat my request of an absolute retraction of all offensive allusions contained therein in relation to my private character and standing.

If you are not the author of any of the articles, your denial will be sufficient. I will say further, it is not my intention to menace, but to do myself justice.

Your ob't serv't,

Jas. Shields.

This Mr. Lincoln perused, and returned to General Whiteside, telling him verbally, that he did not think it consistent with his honor to negotiate for peace with Mr. Shields, unless Mr. Shields would withdraw his former offensive letter.

In a very short time General Whiteside called with a note from Mr. Shields, designating General Whiteside as his friend, to which Mr. Lincoln instantly replied designating me as his. On meeting General Whiteside, he proposed that we should pledge our honor to each other that we would endeavor to settle the matter amicably; to which I agreed, and stated to him the only conditions on which it could be settled; viz., the withdrawal of Mr. Shields's first note, which he appeared to think reasonable, and regretted that the note had been written, saying however, that he had endeavored to prevail on Mr. Shields to write a milder one, but had not succeeded. He added, too, that I must promise not to mention it, as he would not dare to let Mr. Shields know that he was negotiating peace; for, said he, "He would challenge me next, and as soon cut my throat as not." Not willing that he should suppose my principal less dangerous than his own, I promised not to mention our pacific intentions to Mr. Lincoln or any other person; and we started for Springfield forthwith.

We all, except Mr. Shields, arrived in Springfield late at night on Monday. We discovered that the affair had, somehow, got great publicity in Springfield, and that an arrest was probable. To prevent this, it is agreed by Mr. Lincoln and myself that he should leave early on Tuesday morning. Accordingly, he prepared the follownig instructions for my guide, on a suggestion from Mr. Butler that he had reason to believe that an attempt would be made by the opposite party to have the matter accommodated:

In case Whiteside shall signify a wish to adjust this affair without further difficulty, let him know that, if the present papers be withdrawn, and a note from Mr. Shields asking to know if I am the author of the articles of which he complains, and asking that I shall make him gentlemanly satisfaction if I am the author, and this without menace or dictation as to what that satisfaction shall be, a pledge is made that the following answer shall be given:

"I did write the 'Lost Township' letter which appeared in the *Journal* of the 2d inst., but had no participation in any form in any other article alluding to you. I wrote that wholly for political effect. I had no intention of injuring your personal or private character, or standing as a man or a gentleman; and I did not then think, and do not now think, that that article could produce, or has produced, that effect against you; and had I anticipated such an effect, I would have forborne to write it. And I will add, that your conduct towards me, so far as I knew, had always been gentlemanly, and that I had no personal pique against you, and no cause for any."

If this should be done, I leave it with you to manage what shall and what shall not be published.

If nothing like this is done, the preliminaries of the fight are to be:

1st. Weapons:—Cavalry broadswords of the largest size, precisely equal in all respects, and such as now used by the cavalry company at Jacksonville.

2d. Position:—A plank ten feet long, and from nine to twelve inches broad, to be firmly fixed on edge on the ground as the lines between us, which neither is to pass his foot over upon forfeit of his life. Next, a line drawn on the ground on either side of said plank and parallel with it, each at the distance of the whole length of the sword and three feet additional from the plank; and the passing of his own such line by either party during the fight shall be deemed a surrender of the contest.

3d. Time:—On Thursday evening at five o'clock, if you can get it so; but in no case to be at a greater distance of time than Friday evening at 5 o'clock.

4th. Place:—Within three miles of Alton, on the opposite side of the river, the particular spot to be agreed on by you.

Any preliminary details coming within the above rules, you are at liberty to make at your discretion; but you are in no case to swerve from these rules, or to pass beyond their limits.

In the course of the forenoon I met General Whiteside, and he again intimated a wish to adjust the matter amicably. I then read to him Mr. Lincoln's instructions to an adjustment, and the terms of the hostile meeting, if there must be one, both at the same time.

He replied that it was useless to talk of an ad-

justment, if it could only be effected by the withdrawal of Mr. Shield's paper, for such withdrawal
Mr. Shields would never consent to; adding, that
he would as soon think of asking Mr. Shields to
"butt his brains out against a brick wall as to withdraw that paper." He proceeded: "I see but one
course—that is a desperate remedy: 'tis to tell
them, if they will not make the matter up, they
must fight us." I replied, that, if he chose to fight
Mr. Shields to compel him to do right, he might do
so; but as for Mr. Lincoln, he was on the defensive,
and, I believe, in the right, and I should do nothing
to compel him to do wrong. Such withdrawal
having been made indispensable by Mr. Lincoln, I
cut the matter short as to an adjustment, and I
proposed to General Whiteside to accept the terms
of the fight, which he refused to do until Mr. Shields'
arrival in town, but agreed, verbally, that Mr. Lincoln's friends should procure the broadswords, and
take them to the ground. In the afternoon he
came to me, saying that some persons were swear-
ing out affidavits to have us arrested, and that he
intended to meet Mr. Shields immediately, and
proceed to the place designated, lamenting, however, that I would not delay the time, that he might
procure the interference of Governor Ford and General Ewing to mollify Mr. Shields. I told him that
an accommodation, except upon the terms I mentioned, was out of question; that to delay the
meeting was to facilitate our arrest; and, as I was
determined not to be arrested, I should leave the
town in fifteen minutes. I then pressed his acceptance of the preliminaries, which he disclaimed upon
the ground that it would interfere with his oath of
office as Fund Commissioner. I then, with two
other friends, went to Jacksonville, where we joined
Mr. Lincoln about 11 o'clock on Tuesday night.
Wednesday morning we procured the broadswords,

and proceeded to Alton, where we arrived about 11 o'clock A. M., on Thursday. The other party were in town before us. We crossed the river, and they soon followed. Shortly after, General Hardin and Dr. English presented to General Whiteside and myself the following note:

ALTON, September 22, 1842.

MESSRS. WHITESIDE AND MERRYMAN:—As the mutual personal friends of Messrs. Shields and Lincoln, but without authority from either, we earnestly desire to see a reconciliation of the misunderstanding which exists between them. Such difficulties should always be arranged amicably, if it is possible to do so with honor to both parties.

Believing, ourselves, that such an arrangement can possibly be effected, we respectfully but earnestly submit the following proposition for your consideration:

Let the whole difficulty be submitted to four or more gentlemen, to be selected by ourselves, who shall consider the affair, and report thereupon for your consideration.

JOHN J. HARDIN,
R. W. ENGLISH.

To this proposition General Whiteside agreed: I declined doing so without consulting Mr. Lincoln. Mr. Lincoln remarked that, as they had accepted the proposition, he would do so, but directed that his friends should make no terms except those first proposed. Whether the adjustment was finally made upon these very terms and no other, let the following documents attest:

MISSOURI, September 22, 1842.

GENTLEMEN:—All papers in relation to the matter in controversy between Mr. Shields and Mr. Lincoln having been withdrawn by the friends of the parties concerned, the friends of Mr. Shields ask the friends of Mr. Lincoln to explain all offensive matter in the articles which ap-

appeared in the *Sangamon Journal*, of the 2d, 9th, and 16th of September, under the signature of "Rebecca," and headed "Lost Townships."

It is due General Hardin and Mr. English to state that their interference was of the most courteous and gentlemanly character.

JOHN D. WHITESIDE.
WM. LEE D. EWING.
T. M. HOPE.

MISSOURI, September 22, 1842.

GENTLEMEN:—All papers in relation to the matter in controversy between Mr. Lincoln and Mr. Shields having been withdrawn by the friends of the parties concerned, we, the undersigned, friends of Mr. Lincoln, in accordance with your request that explanation of Mr. Lincoln's publication in relation to Mr. Shields in the *Sangamon Journal* of the 2d, 9th, and 16th of September be made, take pleasure in saying, that, although Mr. Lincoln was the writer of the article signed "Rebecca" in the *Journal* of the 2d, and that only, yet he had no intention of injuring the personal or private character or standing of Mr. Shields as a gentleman or a man, and that Mr. Lincoln did not think, nor does he now think, that said article could produce such an effect; and, had Mr. Lincoln anticipated such an effect, he would have forborne to write it. We will state further, that said article was written solely for political effect, and not to gratify any personal pique against Mr. Shields, for he had none and knew of no cause for any. It is due to General Hardin and Mr. English to say that their interference was of the most courteous and gentlemanly character.

E. H. MERRYMAN.
A. T. BLEDSOE.
WM. BUTLER.

Let it be observed now, that Mr. Shields's friends, after agreeing to the arbitrament of four disinterested gentlemen, declined the contract, saying that Mr. Shields wished his own friends to act for him. They then proposed that we should explain without any withdrawal of papers. This was promptly and firmly refused, and general Whiteside himself pronounced the papers withdrawn. They then produced a note requesting us to "disavow" all offensive intentions in the publications, etc., etc. This we declined answering, and only responded to the above requested for an explanation.

These are the material facts in relation to the matter, and I think present the case in a very different light from the garbled and curtailed statment of General Whiteside. Why he made that statement I know not, unless he wished to detract from the honor of Mr. Lincoln. This was ungenerous, more particularly as he on the ground requested us not to make in our explanation any quotations from the "Rebecca papers;" also, not to make public the terms of reconciliation, and to unite with them in defending the honorable character of the adjustment.

General Whiteside, in his publication, says: "The friends of both parties agreed to withdraw the papers (temporarily) to give the friends of Mr. Lincoln an opportunity to explain." This I deny. I say the papers were withdrawn to enable Mr. Shields's friends to ask an explanation; and I appeal to the documents for proof of my position.

By looking over these documents, it will be seen that Mr. Shields had not before asked for an explanation, but had all the time been dictatorially insisting on a retraction.

General Whiteside, in his communication, brings to light much of Mr. Shields's manifestations of bravery behind the scenes. I can do nothing of the kind for Mr. Lincoln. He took his stand when I first met him at Tremont, and maintained it calmly to the last, without difficulty or difference between himself and his friends.

I cannot close this article, lengthly as it is, without testifying to the honorable and gentlemanly conduct of General Ewing and Dr. Hope, nor indeed can I say that I saw anything objectionable in the course of General Whiteside up to the time of his communication. This is so replete with prevarication and misrepresentation, that I cannot accord to the General that candor which I once supposed him to possess. He complains that I did not procrastinate time according to agreement. He forgets that by his own act he cut me off from that chance in inducing me, by promise, not to communicate our secret contract to Mr. Lincoln. Moreover, I could see no consistency in wishing for an extension of time at that stage of the affair, when in the outset they were in so precipitate a hurry that they could not wait three days for Mr. Lincoln to return from Tremont, but must hasten there, apparently with the intention of bringing the matter to a speedy issue. He complains, too, that, after inviting him to take a seat in the buggy I never broached the subject to him on our route here. But was I, the defendant in the case, with a challenge hanging over me, to make advances, and beg a reconciliation?

Absurd! Moreover, the valorous General forgets that he beguiled the tedium of the journey by recounting to me his exploits in many a well-fought battle,—dangers by "flood and field," in which I don't believe he ever participated,—doubtless with a view to produce a salutary effect on my nerves, and impress me with a proper notion of his fire-eating propensities.

One more main point of his argument and I have done. The General seems to be troubled with a convenient shortness of memory on some occasions. He does not remember that any explanations were offered at any time, unless it were a paper read when the "broadsword proposition" was tendered, when his mind was so confused by the anticipated clatter of broadswords, or something else, that he did "not know fully what it purported to be." The truth is, that, by unwisely refraining from mentioning it to his principal, he placed himself in a dilemma which he is now endeavoring to shuffle out of. By his inefficiency and want of knowledge of those laws which govern gentlemen in matters of this kind, he has done great injustice to his principal, a gentleman who, I believe, is ready at all times to vindicate his honor manfully, but who has been unfortunate in the selection of his friends, and this fault he is now trying to wipe out by doing an act of still greater injustice to Mr. Lincoln.

E. H. MERRYMAN.

---

* The following letter from Lincoln to his friend Speed furnishes the final outcome of the "duelling business."

SPRINGFIELD, October 5, 1842.

DEAR SPEED:—

You have heard of my duel with Shields, and I have now to inform you that the duelling business still rages in this city. Day before yesterday Shields challenged Butler, who accepted, proposed fighting next morning at sunrising in Bob Allen's meadow, one hundred yards distance, with rifles. To this Whiteside, Shields's second, said 'no' because of the law. Thus ended duel No. 2. Yesterday Whiteside chose to consider himself insulted by Dr. Merryman, so sent him a kind of quasi-challenge inviting him to meet him at the Planter's House in St. Louis, on the next Friday, to settle their difficulty. Merryman made me his friend, and sent Whiteside a note, inquiring to know if he meant his note as a challenge, and if so, that he would, according to the law in such case made and provided, prescribe the terms of the meeting. Whiteside returned for answer that if Merryman would meet him at the Planter's House as desired, he would challenge him. Merryman replied in a note, that he denied Whiteside's right to dictate time and place, but that he (Merryman) would waive the question of time, and meet him at Louisiana, Mo. Upon my presenting this note to Whiteside, and stating verbally its contents, he declined receiving it, saying he had business in St. Louis, and it was as near as Louisiana. Merryman then directed me to notify Whiteside that he should publish the correspondence between them, with such comments as he saw fit. This I did. Thus it stood at bed-time last night. This morning Whiteside, by his friend Shields, is praying for a new

Dr. Merryman's elaborate and graphic account of
the meeting at the duelling ground and all the preliminary proceedings is as full and complete a history of this serio-comic affair as any historian could
give. Mr. Lincoln, as mentioned in the outset of
this chapter, in the law office and elsewhere, as a
rule, refrained from discussing it. I only remember
of hearing him say this, in reference to the duel:
"I did not intend to hurt Shields unless I did so
clearly in self-defense. If it had been necessary I
could have split him from the crown of his head to
the end of his backbone;" and when one takes into
consideration the conditions of weapons and
position required in his instructions to Dr. Merryman the boast does not seem impossible.

The marriage of Lincoln in no way diminished
his love for politics; in fact, as we shall see later
along, it served to stimulate his zeal in that direction. He embraced every opportunity that offered
for a speech in public. Early in 1842 he entered
into the Washingtonian movement organized to sup-
press the evils of intemperance. At the request of
the society he delivered an admirable address, on
Washington's birthday, in the Presbyterian Church,
which, in keeping with former efforts, has been so
often published that I need not quote it in full. I
was then an ardent temperance reformer myself, and

---

trial, on the ground that he was mistaken in Merryman's proposition to meet him at Louisiana, Mo., thinking it was the State
of Louisiana. This Merryman hoots at, and is preparing his
publication; while the town is in a ferment, and a street-fight
somewhat anticipated. * *

Yours forever,
LINCOLN."

remember well how one paragraph of Lincoln's speech offended the church members who were present. Speaking of certain Christians who objected to the association of drunkards, even with the chance of reforming them, he said: "If they (the Christians) believe, as they profess, that Omnipotence condescended to take on himself the form of sinful man, and as such die an ignominous death, surely they will not refuse submission to the infinitely lesser condescension, for the temporal and perhaps eternal salvation of a large, erring, and unfortunate class of their fellow-creatures. Nor is the condescension very great. In my judgment such of us as have never fallen victims have been spared more from the absence of appetite than from any mental or moral superiority over those who have. Indeed, I believe, if we take habitual drunkards as a class, their heads and their hearts will bear an advantageous comparison with those of any other class." The avowal of these sentiments proved to be an unfortunate thing for Lincoln. The professing Christians regarded the suspicion suggested in the first sentence as a reflection on the sincerity of their belief, and the last one had no better effect in reconciling them to his views. I was at the door of the church as the people passed out, and heard them discussing the speech. Many of them were open in the expression of their displeasure. "It's a shame," I heard one man say, "that he should be permitted to abuse us so in the house of the Lord." The truth was the society was composed mainly of the roughs and drunkards of the town, who had evinced a desire

to reform. Many of them were too fresh from the
gutter to be taken at once into the society of such
people as worshipped at the church where the
speech was delivered. Neither was there that
concert of effort so universal to-day between the
churches and temperance societies to rescue the
fallen. The whole thing, I repeat, was damaging to
Lincoln, and gave rise to the opposition on the
part of the churches which confronted him several
years afterwards when he became a candidate against
the noted Peter Cartwright for Congress. The
charge, therefore, that in matters of religion he was
a skeptic was not without its supporters, especially
where his opponent was himself a preacher. But,
nothing daunted, Lincoln kept on and labored
zealously in the interest of the temperance movement. He spoke often again in Springfield, and
also in other places over the country, displaying
the same courage and adherence to principle that
characterized his every undertaking.

Meanwhile, he had one eye open for politics as he
moved along. He was growing more self-reliant in
the practice of law every day, and felt amply able to
take charge of and maintain himself in any case
that happened to come into his hands. His propensity for the narration of an apt story was of immeasurable aid to him before a jury, and in cases
where the law seemed to lean towards the other
side won him many a case. In 1842, Martin Van
Buren, who had just left the Presidential chair, made
a journey through the West. He was accompanied
by his former Secretary of the Navy, Mr. Paulding,

and in June they reached the village of Rochester, distant from Springfield six miles. It was evening when they arrived, and on account of the muddy roads they decided to go no farther, but to rest there for the night. Word was sent into Springfield, and of course the leading Democrats of the capital hurried out to meet the distinguished visitor. Knowing the accommodations at Rochester were not intended for or suited to the entertainment of an ex-President, they took with them refreshments in quantity and variety, to make up for all deficiencies. Among others, they prevailed on Lincoln, although an ardent and pronounced Whig, to accompany them. They introduced him to the venerable statesman of Kinderhook as a representative lawyer, and a man whose wit was as ready as his store of anecdotes was exhaustless. How he succeeded in entertaining the visitor and the company, those who were present have often since testified. Van Buren himself entertained the crowd with reminiscences of politics in New York, going back to the days of Hamilton and Burr, and many of the crowd in turn interested him with graphic descriptions of early life on the western frontier. But they all yielded at last to the piquancy and force of Lincoln's queer stories. "Of these," relates one of the company,* "there was a constant supply, one following another in rapid succession, each more irresistible than its predecessor. The fun continued until after midnight, and until the distinguished traveller insisted that

---

* Jos. Gillespie, MS. letter, September 6, 1866.

his sides were sore from laughing." The yarns
which Lincoln gravely spun out, Van Buren assured
the crowd, he never would forget.

After April 14, 1841, when Lincoln retired from
the partnership with Stuart, who had gone to Congress, he had been associated with Stephen T.
Logan, a man who had, as he deserved, the reputation of being the best *nisi prius* lawyer in the State.
Judge Logan was a very orderly but somewhat
technical lawyer. He had some fondness for politics, and made one race for Congress, but he lacked
the elements of a successful politician. He was defeated, and returned to the law. He was assiduous
in study and tireless in search of legal principles.
He was industrious and very thrifty, delighted to
make and save money, and died a rich man. Lincoln had none of Logan's qualities. He was anything but studious, and had no money sense. He
was five years younger, and yet his mind and make-
up so impressed Logan that he was invited into the
partnership with him. Logan's example had a good
effect on Lincoln, and it stimulated him to unusual
endeavors. For the first time he realized the effectiveness of order and method in work, but his old
habits eventually overcame him. He permitted his
partner to do all the studying in the preparation of
cases, while he himself trusted to his general knowledge of the law and the inspiration of the surroundings to overcome the judge or the jury. Logan
was scrupulously exact, and used extraordinary care
in the preparation of papers. His words were well
chosen, and his style of composition was stately and

formal. This extended even to his letters. This
Lincoln lacked in every particular. I have before
me a letter written by Lincoln at this time to the
proprietors of a wholesale store in Louisville, for
whom suit had been brought, in which, after notify-
ing the latter of the sale of certain real estate in
satisfaction of their judgment, he adds: "As to
the real estate we cannot attend to it. We are not
real estate agents, we are lawyers. We recommend
that you give the charge of it to Mr. Isaac S.
Britton, a trustworthy man, and one whom the
Lord made on purpose for such business." He
gravely signs the firm name, Logan and Lincoln, to
this unlawyerlike letter and sends it on its way.
Logan never would have written such a letter. He
had too much gravity and austere dignity to permit
any such looseness of expression in letters to his
clients or to anyone else.

In 1843, Logan and Lincoln both had their eyes
set on the race for Congress. Logan's claim to the
honor lay in his age and the services he had rendered the Whig party, while Lincoln, overflowing
with ambition, lay great stress on his legislative
achievements, and demanded it because he had
been defeated in the nominating conventions by
both Hardin and Baker in the order named. That
two such aspiring politicians, each striving to obtain
the same prize, should not dwell harmoniously
together in the same office is not strange. Indeed,
we may reasonably credit the story that they considered themselves rivals, and that numerous sacri-
monious passages took place between them. I was

not surprised, therefore, one morning, to see Mr. Lincoln come rushing up into my quarters and with more or less agitation tell me he had determined to sever the partnership with Logan. I confess I was surprised when he invited me to become his partner. I was young in the practice and was painfully aware of my want of ability and experience; but when he remarked in his earnest, honest way, "Billy, I can trust you, if you can trust me," I felt relieved, and accepted the generous proposal. It has always been a matter of pride with me that during our long partnership, continuing on until it was dissolved by the bullet of the assassin Booth, we never had any personal controversy or disagreement. I never stood in his way for political honors or office, and I believe we understood each other perfectly. In after years, when he became more prominent, and our practice grew to respectable proportions, other ambitious practitioners undertook to supplant me in the partnership. One of the latter, more zealous than wise, charged that I was in a certain way weakening the influence of the firm. I am flattered to know that Lincoln turned on this last named individual with the retort, "I know my own business, I reckon. I know Billy Herndon better than anybody, and even if what you say of him is true I intend to stick by him."

Lincoln's effort to obtain the Congressional nomination in 1843 brought out several unique and amusing incidents. He and Edward D. Baker were the two aspirants from Sangamon county, but Baker's long residence, extensive acquaintance, and general popularity were obstacles Lincoln could not overcome; accordingly, at the last moment, Lincoln reluctantly withdrew from the field. In a letter to his friend Speed, dated March 24, 1843, he describes the situation as follows: "We had a meeting of the Whigs of the county here on last Monday, to appoint delegates to a district convention; and Baker beat me, and got the delegation instructed to go for him. The meeting, in spite of my attempt to decline it, appointed me one of the delegates; so that in getting Baker the nomination I shall be fixed a good deal like a fellow who is made groomsman to a man that has cut him out, and is marrying his own dear gal." Only a few days before this he had written a friend anent the Congressional matter, "Now if you should hear any one say that Lincoln don't want to go to Congress, I wish you, as a personal friend of mine, would tell him you have reason to believe he is mistaken. The truth is I would like to go very much. Still, circumstances may happen which may prevent my being a candidate. If there are any who be my friends in such an enterprise, what I now want is that they shall not throw me away just yet."* To another friend in the adjoining county of Menard a few days after the meeting of the Whigs in Sangamon, he explains how Baker defeated him.

The entire absence of any feeling of bitterness, or what the politicians call revenge, is the most striking feature of the letter. "It is truly gratify-

* Letter to R. S. Thomas, Virginia, Ill., Feb. 14, '43, MS.

ing," he says, "to me to learn that while the people of Sangamon have cast me off, my old friends
of Menard, who have known me longest and best,
stick to me. It would astonish if not amuse the
older citizens to learn that I (a strange, friendless,
unedutated, penniless boy, working on a flat-boat at
ten dollars per month) have been put down
here as the candidate of pride, wealth, and aristocratic family distinction. Yet so, chiefly, it was.
There was, too, the strangest combination of
church influence against me. Baker is a Campbell-
ite, and therefore as I suppose, with few excep-
tions, got all that church. My wife has some
relations in the Presbyterian churches and some
with the Episcopalian churches, and therefore,
wherever it would tell, I was set down as either the
one or the other, while it was everywhere contended
that no Christian ought to go for me, because I
belonged to no church, was suspected of being a
deist, and had talked about fighting a duel. With
all these things Baker, of course, had nothing to
do; nor do I complain of them. As to his own
church going for him I think that was right enough;
and as to the influences I have spoken of in the
other, though they were very strong, it would be
grossly untrue and unjust to charge that they acted
upon them in a body, or were very near so. I only
mean that those influences levied a tax of considerable per cent. and throughout the religious controversy." To a proposition offering to instruct
the Menard delegation for him he replies: "You
say you shall instruct your delegates for me unless

I object. I certainly shall not object. That would be too pleasant a compliment for me to tread in the dust. And besides, if anything should happen (which, however, is not probable) by which Baker should be thrown out of the fight, I would be at liberty to accept the nomination if I could get it. I do, however, feel myself bound not to hinder him in any way from getting the nomination. I should despise myself were I to attempt it."

Baker's friends had used as an argument against Lincoln that he belonged to a proud and aristocratic family, referring doubtless to some of the distinguished relatives who were connected with him by marriage. The story reaching Lincoln's ears, he laughed heartily over it one day in a Springfield store and remarked:

"That sounds strange to me, for I do not remember of but one who ever came to see me, and while he was in town he was accused of stealing a jew's-harp."* In the convention which was held shortly after at the town of Pekin neither Baker nor Lincoln obtained the coveted honor; but John J. Hardin, of Morgan, destined to lose his life at the head of an Illinois regiment in the Mexican war, was nominated, and in the following August, elected by a good majority. Lincoln bore his defeat manfully. He was no doubt greatly disappointed, but by no means soured. He conceived the strange notion that the publicity given his so-called "aristocratic family distinction" would cost him the friendship of his humbler constituents—his Clary's Grove

* Letter, A. Y. Ellis, July 16, '66, MS.

friends. He took his friend James Matheney out
into the woods with him one day and, calling up the
bitter features of the canvass, protested "vehemently
and with great emphasis" that he was anything
but aristocratic and proud. "Why, Jim," he said,
"I am now and always shall be the same Abe
Lincoln I was when you first saw me."

In the campaign of 1844 Lincoln filled the honorable post of Presidential Elector, and he extended
the limits of his acquaintance by stumping the
State. This was the year the gallant and magnetic
Clay went down in defeat. Lincoln, in the latter
end of the canvass, crossed over into Indiana and
made several speeches. He spoke at Rockport and
also at Gentryville, where he met the Grigsbys, the
Gentrys, and other friends of his boyhood.   The
result of the election was a severe disappointment
to Mr. Lincoln as well as to all other Whigs. No
election since the foundation of the Government
created more widespread regret than the defeat of
Clay by Polk. Men were never before so enlisted
in any man's cause, and when the great Whig chief-
tain went down his followers fled from the field in
utter demoralization. Some doubted the success of
popular government, while others, more hopeful
still in the face of the general disaster, vowed they
would never shave their faces or cut their hair till
Henry Clay became President. As late as 1880 I saw
one man who had lived up to his insane resolution.
One political society organized to aid Clay's election sent the defeated candidate an address, in which
they assured him that, after the smoke of ·battle

had cleared away, he would ever be remembered
as one "whose name honored defeat and gave it a
glory which victory could not have brought." In
Lincoln's case his disappointment was no greater
than that of any other Whig. Many persons have
yielded to the impression that Mr. Lincoln visited
Clay at his home in Lexington and felt a personal
loss in his defeat, but such is not the case. He
took no more gloomy view of the situation than
the rest of his party. He had been a leading figure
himself in other campaigns, and was fully inured
to the chilling blasts of defeat. They may have
driven him in, but only for a short time, for he soon
evinced a willingness to test the temper of the
winds again.

No sooner had Baker been elected to Congress in
August, 1844, than Lincoln began to manifest a
longing for the tempting prize to be contended for
in 1846. Hardin and Baker both having been
required to content themselves with a single term
each, the struggle among Whig aspirants narrowed
down to Logan and Lincoln.* The latter's claim

---

* The Whig candidates for Congress in the Springfield district
"rotated" in the following order: Baker succeeded Hardin in
1844, Lincoln was elected in 1846, and Logan was nominated but
defeated in 1848. Lincoln publicly declined to contest the nomination with Baker in 1844; Hardin did the same for Lincoln in
1846—although both seem to have acted reluctantly; and Lincoln refused to run against Logan in 1848. Many persons insist that an agreement among these four conspicuous Whig
leaders to content themselves with one term each actually existed. There is, however, no proof of any bargain, although
there seems to have been a tacit understanding of the kind—
maintained probably to keep other and less tractable candidates
out of the field.

seemed to find such favorable lodgment with the
party workers, and his popularity seemed so apparent, that Logan soon realized his own want of
strength and abandoned the field to his late law
partner. The convention which nominated Lincoln
met at Petersburg May 1, 1846. Hardin, who, in
violation of what was then regarded as precedent,
had been seeking the nomination, had courteously
withdrawn. Logan, ambitious to secure the honor
next time for himself, with apparent generosity
presented Lincoln's name to the convention, and
there being no other candidate he was chosen unani-
mously. The reader need not be told whom the
Democrats placed in the field against him. It was
Peter Cartwright, the famous Methodist divine and
circuit rider. An energetic canvass of three months
followed, during which Lincoln kept his forces well
in hand. He was active and alert, speaking everywhere, and abandoning his share of business in the
law office entirely. He had a formidable competitor in Cartwright, who not only had an extensive
following by reason of his church influence, but
rallied many more supporters around his standard
by his pronounced Jacksonian attitude. He had
come into Illinois with the early immigrants from
Kentucky and Tennessee, and had at one time or
another preached to almost every Methodist con-
gregation between Springfield and Cairo. He had
extensive family connections all over the district,
was almost twenty-five years older than Lincoln,
and in every respect a dangerous antagonist.
Another thing which operated much to Lincoln's

disadvantage was the report circulated by Cartwright's friends with respect to Lincoln's religious
views. He was charged with the grave offence of
infidelity, and sentiments which he was reported to
have expressed with reference to the inspiration of
the Bible were given the campaign varnish and
passed from hand to hand. His slighting allusion
expressed in the address at the Presbyterian Church
before the Washington Temperance Society, February 2d, four years before, to the insincerity of the
Christian people was not forgotten. It, too, played
its part; but all these opposing circumstances were
of no avail. Cartwright was personally very popular, but it was plain the people of the Springfield
district wanted no preacher to represent them in
Congress. They believed in an absolute separation
of Church and State. The election, therefore, of
such a man as Cartwright would not, to their way of
thinking, tend to promote such a result. I was
enthusiastic and active in Lincoln's interest myself.
The very thought of my associate's becoming a member of Congress was a great stimulus to my self-
importance. Many other friends in and around
Springfield were equally as vigilant, and, in the
language of another, "long before the contest closed
we snuffed approaching victory in the air." Our
laborious efforts met with a suitable reward. Lincoln was elected by a majority of 1511 in the district, a larger vote than Clay's two years before,
which was only 914. In Sangamon county his
majority was 690, and exceeded that of any of his
predecessors on the Whig ticket, commencing with

Stuart in 1834 and continuing on down to the days of Yates in 1852.

Before Lincoln's departure for Washington to enter on his duties as a member of Congress, the Mexican war had begun. The volunteers had gone forward, and at the head of the regiments from Illinois some of the bravest men and the best legal talent in Springfield had marched. Hardin, Baker, Bissell, and even the dramatic Shields had enlisted. The issues of the war and the manner of its prosecution were in every man's mouth. Naturally, therefore, a Congressman-elect would be expected to publish his views and define his position early in the day. Although, in common with the Whig party, opposing the declaration of war, Lincoln, now that hostilities had commenced, urges a vigorous prosecution. He admonished us all to permit our Government to suffer no dishonor, and to stand by the flag till peace came and came honorably to us. He declared these sentiments in a speech at a public meeting in Springfield, May 29, 1847. In the following December he took his seat in Congress. He was the only Whig from Illinois. His colleagues in the Illinois delegation were John A. McClernand, O. B. Ficklin, William A. Richardson, Thomas J. Turner, Robert Smith, and John Wentworth. In the Senate Douglas had made his appearance for the first time. The Little Giant is always in sight! Robert C. Winthrop, of Massachusetts, was chosen Speaker. John Quincy Adams, Horace Mann, Caleb Smith, Alexander H. Stephens, Robert Toombs, Howell Cobb, and

Andrew Johnson were important members of the House. With many of these the newly elected member from Illinois was destined to sustain another and far different relation.

On the 5th of December, the day before the House organized, Lincoln wrote me a letter about our fee in a law-suit and reported the result of the Whig caucus the night before. On the 13th, he wrote again: "Dear William:—Your letter, advising me of the receipt of our fee in the bank case, is just received, and I don't expect to hear another as good a piece of news from Springfield while I am away." He then directed me from the proceeds of this fee to pay a debt at the bank, and out of the balance left to settle sundry dry-goods and grocery bills. The modest tone of the last paragraph is its most striking feature. "As you are all so anxious for me to distinguish myself," he said, "I have concluded to do so before long." January 8 he writes: "As to speech-making, by way of getting the hang of the House, I made a little speech two or three days ago on a post-office question of no general interest. I find speaking here and elsewhere about the same thing. I was about as badly scared, and no worse, as I am when I speak in court. I expect to make one within a week or two in which I hope to succeed well enough to wish you to see it." Meanwhile, in recognition of the assurances I had sent him from friends who desired to approve his course by a re-election, he says: "It is very pleasant to me to learn from you that there are some who desire that I should be re-elected. I

most heartily thank them for the kind partiality,
and I can say, as Mr. Clay said of the annexation of
Texas, that, 'personally, I would not object' to a
re-election, although I thought at the time, and
still think, it would be quite as well for me to
return to the law at the end of a single term. I
made the declaration that I would not be a candidate again, more from a wish to deal fairly with
others, to keep peace among our friends, and to
keep the district from going to the enemy, than for
any cause personal to myself, so that if it should
happen that nobody else wishes to be elected I
could not refuse the people the right of sending
me again. But to enter myself as a competitor of
others, or to authorize any one so to enter me, is
what my word and honor forbid."

His announcement of a willingness to accept a
re-election if tendered him by the people was
altogether unnecessary, for within a few days after
this letter was written his constituents began to
manifest symptoms of grave disapproval of his
course on the Mexican war question. His position
on this subject was evidenced by certain resolutions
offered by him in the House three weeks before.
These latter were called the "Spot Resolutions,"
and they and the speech which followed on the 12th
of January in support of them not only sealed
Lincoln's doom as a Congressman, but in my
opinion, lost the district to the Whigs in 1848,
when Judge Logan had succeeded at last in obtaining the nomination.

Although differing with the President as to the

justice or even propriety of a war with Mexico, Lincoln was not unwilling to vote, and with the majority of his party did vote, the supplies necessary to carry it on. He did this, however, with great reluctance, protesting all the while that "the war was unnecessarily and unconstitutionally begun by the President." The "Spot Resolutions," which served as a text for his speech on the 12th of January, and which caused such unwonted annoyance in the ranks of his constituents, were a series following a preamble loaded with quotations from the President's messages. These resolutions requested the President to inform the House: *"First.* Whether the *spot* on which the blood of our citizens was shed as in his messages declared was or was not within the territory of Spain, at least after the treaty of 1819, until the Mexican revolution. *Second.* Whether that spot is or is not within the territory which was wrested from Spain by the revolutionary government of Mexico. *Third.* Whether that spot is or is not within a settlement of people, which settlement has existed ever since long before the Texas revolution, and until its inhabitants fled before the approach of the United States army." There were eight of these interrogatories, but it is only necessary to reproduce the three which foreshadow the position Lincoln was then intending to assume. On the 12th of January, as before stated, he followed them up with a carefully prepared and well arranged speech, in which he made a severe arraignment of President Polk and justified the pertinence and propriety of the inquiries he had a few

days before addressed to him. The speech is too
long for insertion here. It was constructed much
after the manner of a legal argument. Reviewing
the evidence furnished by the President in his
various messages, he undertook to "smoke him
out" with this: "Let the President answer the
interrogatories I proposed, as before mentioned, or
other similar ones. Let him answer fully, fairly,
candidly. Let him answer with facts, not with
arguments. Let him remember, he sits where
Washington sat; and so remembering, let him
answer as Washington would answer. As a nation
should not, and the Almighty will not, be evaded,
so let him attempt no evasion, no equivocation.
And if, so answering, he can show the soil was ours
where the first blood of the war was shed; that it
was not within an inhabited country, or if within
such; that the inhabitants had submitted themselves
to the civil authority of Texas or of the United
States; and that the same is true of the site of Fort
Brown, then I am with him for his justification . . .
But if he cannot or will not do this—if, on any
pretence, or no pretence, he shall refuse or omit it
—then I shall be fully convinced of what I more
than suspect already—that he is deeply conscious
of being in the wrong; that he feels the blood of
this war, like the blood of Abel, is crying to Heaven
against him; that he ordered General Taylor into
the midst of a peaceful Mexican settlement purposely to bring on a war; that, originally having
some strong motive—which I will not now stop to
give my opinion concerning—to involve the coun-

tries in a war, and trusting to escape scrutiny by fixing the public gaze upon the exceeding brightness of military glory,—that attractive rainbow that rises in showers of blood, that serpent's eye that charms to destroy,—he plunged into it, and has swept on and on, till disappointed in his calculation of the ease with which Mexico might be subdued, he now finds himself he knows not where. He is a bewildered, confounded, and miserably perplexed man. God grant that he may be able to show that there is not something about his conscience more painful than all his mental perplexity." This speech, however clear may have been its reasoning, however rich in illustration, in restrained and burning earnestness, yet was unsuccessful in "smoking out" the President. He remained within the official seclusion his position gave him, and declined to answer. In fact it is doubtless true that Lincoln anticipated no response, but simply took that means of defining clearly his own position.

On the 19th inst., having occasion to write me with reference to a note with which one of our clients, one Louis Candler, had been "annoying" him, "not the least of which annoyance," he complains, "is his cursed unreadable and ungodly handwriting," he adds a line, in which with noticeable modesty he informs me: "I have made a speech, a copy of which I send you by mail." He doubtless felt he was taking rather advanced and perhaps questionable ground. And so he was, for very soon after, murmurs of dissatisfaction began to run through the Whig ranks. I did not, as some of Lincoln's biographers would have their readers believe, inaugurate this feeling of dissatisfaction. On the contrary, as the law partner of the Congressman, and as his ardent admirer, I discouraged the defection all I could. Still, when I listened to the comments of his friends everywhere after the delivery of his speech, I felt that he had made a mistake. I therefore wrote him to that effect, at the same time giving him my own views, which I knew were in full accord with the views of his Whig constituents. My argument in substance was: That the President of the United States is Commander-in-Chief of the Army and Navy; that as such commander it was his duty, in the absence of Congress, if the country was about to be invaded and armies were organized in Mexico for that purpose, to go —if necessary—into the very heart of Mexico and prevent the invasion. I argued further that it would be a crime in the Executive to let the country be invaded in the least degree. The action of the President was a necessity, and under a similar necessity years afterward Mr. Lincoln himself emancipated the slaves, although he had no special power under the Constitution to do so. In later days, in what is called the Hodges letter, concerning the freedom of the slaves, he used this language:

"I felt that measures otherwise unconstitutional might become lawful by becoming indispensable."

Briefly stated, that was the strain of my argument. My judgment was formed on the law of nations and of war. If the facts were as I believed them, and my premises correct, then I assumed that the President's acts became lawful by becoming indispensable.

February 1 he wrote me, "Dear William: You fear that you and I disagree about the war. I regret this, not because of any fear we shall remain disagreed after you have read this letter, but because if you misunderstand I fear other good friends may also."

Speaking of his vote in favor of the amendment to the supply bill proposed by George Ashmun, of Massachusetts, he continues:

"That vote affirms that the war was unnecessarily and unconstitutionally commenced by the President; and I will stake my life that if you had been in my place you would have voted just as I did. Would you have voted what you felt and knew to be a lie? I know you would not. Would you have gone out of the House,—skulked the vote? I expect not. If you had skulked one vote you would have had to skulk many more before the close of the session. Richardson's resolutions, introduced before I made any move or gave any vote upon the subject, make the direct question of the justice of the war; so that no man can be silent if he would. You are compelled to speak; and your only alternative is to tell the truth or tell a lie. I cannot doubt which you would do . . . I do not mean this letter for the public, but for you. Before it reaches you you will have seen and read my pamphlet speech and perhaps have been scared anew by it. After you get over your scare read it over again, sentence by sentence, and tell me honestly what you think of it. I condensed all I could for fear of being cut off by the hour rule; and when I got through I had spoken but forty-five minutes.

"Yours forever,

"A. LINCOLN."

I digress from the Mexican war subject long enough to insert, because in the order of time it belongs here, a characteristic letter which he wrote me regarding a man who was destined at a later day to play a far different role in the national drama. Here it is:

"WASHINGTON, Feb. 2, 1848.

"DEAR WILLIAM:

"I just take up my pen to say that Mr. Stephens, of Georgia, a little, slim, pale-faced, consumptive man, with a voice like Logan's, has just concluded the very best speech of an hour's length I ever heard. My old, withered, dry eyes are full of tears yet. If he writes it out anything like he delivered it our people shall see a good many copies of it.

"Yours truly,

"A. LINCOLN."

To WM. H. HERNDON, ESQ.

February 15 he wrote me again in criticism of the President's invasion of foreign soil. He still believed the Executive had exceeded the limit of his authority. "The provision of the Constitution giving the war-making power to Congress," he insists, "was dictated, as I understand it, by the following reasons: kings had always been involving and impoverishing their people in wars, pretending generally, if not always, that the good of the people was the object. This, our convention understood to be the most oppressive of all kingly oppressions; and they resolved to so frame the Constitution that no one man should hold the power of bringing this oppression upon us. But your view destroys the whole matter, and places our President where kings have always stood."

In June the Whigs met in national convention at Philadelphia to nominate a candidate for President. Lincoln attended as a delegate. He advocated the nomination of Taylor because of his belief that he could be elected, and was correspondingly averse to Clay because of the latter's signal defeat in 1844. In a letter from Washington a few days after the convention he predicts the election of "Old Rough." He says: "In my opinion we shall have a most overwhelming glorious triumph. One unmistakable sign is that all the odds and ends are with us—Barn-burners, Native Americans, Tylermen, disappointed office-seeking Locofocos, and the Lord knows what not . . . Taylor's nomination takes the Locos on the blind side. It turns the war thunder against them. The war is now to them the gallows of Haman, which they built for us and on which they are doomed to be hanged themselves."

Meanwhile, in spite of the hopeful view Lincoln seemed to take of the prospect, things in his own district were in exceedingly bad repair. I could not refrain from apprising him of the extensive defections from the party ranks, and the injury his course was doing him. My object in thus writing to him was not to threaten him. Lincoln was not a man who could be successfully threatened; one had to approach him from a different direction. I warned him of public disappointment over his course, and I earnestly desired to prevent him from committing what I believed to be political suicide. June 22d he answered a letter I had written him on the 15th. He had just returned from a Whig caucus held in relation to the coming Presidential election. "The whole field of the nation was scanned; all is high hope and confidence," he said exultingly. "Illinois is expected to better her condition in this race. Under these circumstances judge how heart-rending it was to come to my room and find and read your discouraging letter of the 15th." But still he does not despair. "Now, as to the young men," he says, "you must not wait to be brought forward by the older men. For instance, do you suppose that I should ever have got into notice if I had waited to be hunted up and pushed forward by older men? You young men get together and form a Rough and Ready club, and have regular meetings and speeches. Take in everybody that you can get . . . As you go along gather up all the shrewd, wild boys about town, whether just of age or a little under age. Let every one play the part he can play best—some speak, some sing, and all halloo. Your meetings will be of evenings; the older men and the women will go to hear you, so that it will not only contribute to the election of 'Old Zack,' but will be an interesting pastime and improving to the faculties of all engaged." He was evidently endeavoring through me to rouse up all the enthusiasm among the youth of Springfield possible under the circumstances. But I was disposed to take a dispirited view of the situation, and therefore was not easily warmed up. I felt at this time, somewhat in advance of its occurrence, the death throes of the Whig party. I did not conceal my suspicions, and one of the Springfield papers gave my sentiments liberal quotation in its columns. I felt gloomy over the prospect, and cut out these newspaper slips and sent them to Lincoln. Accompanying these I wrote him a letter equally melancholy in tone, in which among other things I reflected severely on the stubbornness and bad judgment of the old· fossils in the party, who were constantly holding the young men back. This brought from him a letter, July 10, 1848, which is so clearly Lincolnian and so full of plain philosophy, that I copy it in full. Not the least singular of all is his illusion to himself as an old man, although he had scarcely passed his thirty-ninth year.

"WASHINGTON, July 10, 1848.

"DEAR WILLIAM:

"Your letter covering the newspaper slips was received last night. The subject of that letter is exceedingly painful to me, and I cannot but think there is some mistake in your impression of the motives of the old men. I suppose I am now one of the old men; and I declare on my veracity, which I think is good with you, that nothing could afford me more satisfaction than to learn that you and others of my young friends at home were doing battle in the contest and endearing themselves to the people and taking a stand far above any I have ever been able to reach in their admiration. I cannot conceive that other men feel differently. Of course I cannot demonstrate what I say; but I was young once, and I am sure I was never ungenerously thrust back. I hardly know

what to say. The way for a young man to rise is
to improve himself every way he can, never suspect-
ing that anybody wishes to hinder him. Allow me
to assure you that suspicion and jealousy never did
help any man in any situation. There may sometimes be ungenerous attempts to keep a young man
down; and they will succeed, too, if he allows his
mind to be diverted from its true channel to brood
over the attempted injury. Cast about and see if
this feeling has not injured every person you have
ever known to fall into it.

"Now, in what I have said I am sure you will suspect nothing but sincere friendship. I would save
you from a fatal error. You have been a laborious,
studious young man. You are far better informed
on almost all subjects than I ever have been. You
cannot fail in any laudable object unless you allow
your mind to be improperly directed. I have some
the advantage of you in the world's experience
merely by being older; and it is this that induces
me to advise.

"Your friend, as ever,

"A. LINCOLN."

Before the close of the Congressional session he
made two more speeches. One of these, which he
hastened to send home in pamphlet form, and which
he supposes "nobody will read," was devoted to
the familiar subject of internal improvements, and
deserves only passing mention. The other, delivered on the 27th of July, was in its way a masterpiece; and it is no stretch of the truth to say that
while intended simply as a campaign document and
devoid of any effort at classic oratory, it was, perhaps, one of the best speeches of the session. It is
too extended for insertion here without abridgment;

but one who reads it will lay it down convinced that Lincoln's ascendency for a quarter of a century among the political spirits in Illinois was by no means an accident; neither will the reader wonder that Douglas, with all his forensic ability, averted, as long as he could, a contest with a man whose plain, analytical reasoning was not less potent than his mingled drollery and caricature were effective. The speech in the main is an arraignment of General Cass, the Democratic candidate for President, who had already achieved great renown in the political world, principally on account of his career as a soldier in the war of 1812, and is a triumphant vindication of his Whig opponent, General Taylor, who seemed to have had a less extensive knowledge of civil than of military affairs, and was discreetly silent about both. Lincoln caricatured the military pretentions of the Democratic candidate in picturesque style. This latter section of the speech has heretofore been omitted by most of Mr. Lincoln's biographers because of its glaring inappropriateness as a Congressional effort. I have always failed to see wherein its comparison with scores of others delivered in the halls of Congress since that time could in any way detract from the fame of Mr. Lincoln, and I therefore reproduce it here:

"But the gentlemen from Georgia [Mr. Iverson] further says, we have deserted all our principles, and taken shelter under General Taylor's military coat-tail; and he seems to think this is exceedingly degrading. Well, as his faith is, so be it unto him. But can he remember no other military coat-tail,

under which a certain other party have been shelter-
ing for near a quarter of a century? Has he no acquaintance with the ample military coat-tail of General Jackson? Does he not know that his own party
have run the last five Presidential races under that
coat-tail? and that they are now running the sixth
under the same cover? Yes, sir, that coat-tail was
used not only for General Jackson himself, but has
been clung to with the grip of death by every Democratic candidate since. You have never ventured,
and dare not now venture from under it. Your campaign papers have constantly been 'Old Hickory's',
with rude likeness of the old general upon them;
hickory poles and hickory brooms your never-ending
emblems. Mr. Polk himself was 'Young Hickory,'
'Little Hickory,' or something so; and even now
your campaign paper here is proclaiming that Cass
and Butler are of the 'Hickory stripe.' No, sir, you
dare not give it up. Like a horde of hungry ticks,
you have stuck to the tail of the Hermitage lion to
the end of his life; and you are still sticking to it,
and drawing a loathsome sustenance from it, after
he is dead. A fellow once advertised that he had
made a discovery by which he could make a new
man out of an old one and have enough of the stuff
left to make a little yellow dog. Just such a discovery has General Jackson's popularity been to
you. You not only twice made Presidents of him
out of it, but you have enough of the stuff left to
make Presidents of several comparatively small men
since; and it is your chief reliance now to make still
another.

"Mr. Speaker, old horses and military coat-tails,
or tails of any sort, are not figures of speech such
as I would be the first to introduce into discussion
here; but as the gentleman from Georgia has
thought fit to introduce them, he and you are wel-
come to all you have made or can make by them.

If you have any more old horses, trot them out; any more tails, just cock them and come at us. I repeat, I would not introduce this mode of discussion here; but I wish gentlemen on the other side to understand that the use of degrading figures is a game at which they may find themselves unable to take all the winnings. [A voice 'No, we give it up'] Aye! you give it up, and well you may; but for a very different reason from that which you would have us understand. The point—the power to hurt—of all figures consists in the truthfulness of their application; and, understanding this, you may well give it up. They are weapons which hit you, but miss us.

"But in my hurry I was very near closing on this subject of military tails before I was done with it. There is one entire article of the sort I have not discussed yet; I mean the military tail you Democrats are now engaged in dovetailing on to the great Michigander. Yes, sir, all his biographers (and they are legion) have him in hand, tying him to a military tail, like so many mischievous boys tying a dog to a bladder of beans. True, the material is very limited, but they are at it might and main. He invaded Canada without resistance, and he outvaded it without pursuit. As he did both under orders, I suppose there was to him neither credit nor discredit; but they are made to constitute a large part of the tail. He was not at Hull's surrender, but he was close by; he was volunteer aid to General Harrison on the day of the battle of the Thames; and as you said in 1840 Harrison was picking whortleberries two miles off while the battle was fought, I suppose it is a just conclusion with you to say Cass was aiding Harrison to pick whortleberries. This is about all, except the mooted question of the broken sword. Some authors say he broke it; some say he threw it away;

and some others, who ought to know, say nothing about it. Perhaps it would be a fair historical compromise to say if he did not break it, he did not do anything else with it.

"By the way, Mr. Speaker, did you know I am a military hero? Yes, sir, in the days of the Black Hawk war, I fought, bled, and came away. Speaking of General Cass's career, reminds me of my own. I was not at Stillman's defeat, but I was about as near it as Cass was to Hull's surrender; and, like him, I saw the place very soon afterward. It is quite certain I did not break my sword, for I had none to break, but I bent my musket pretty badly on one occasion. If Cass broke his sword, the idea is, he broke it in desparation; I bent the musket by accident. If General Cass went in advance of me picking whortleberries, I guess I surpassed him in charges upon the wild onions. If he saw any live fighting Indians, it was more than I did, but I had a good many bloody struggles with the mosquitos; and, although I never fainted from loss of blood, I can truly say I was often very hungry. Mr. Speaker, if ever I should conclude to doff whatever our Democratic friends may suppose there is of black-cockade Federalism about me, and, thereupon they shall take me up as their candidate for the Presidency, I protest that they shall not make fun of me as they have of General Cass by attempting to write me into a military hero."

After the adjournment of Congress on the 14th of August, Lincoln went through New York and some of the New England States making a number of speeches for Taylor, none of which, owing to the limited facilities attending newspaper reporting in that day, have been preserved. He returned to Illinois before the close of the canvass and continued his efforts on the stump till the election. At the second session of Congress, which began in December, he was less conspicuous than before. The few weeks spent with his constituents had perhaps taught him that in order to succeed as a Congress-man it is not always the most politic thing to tell the truth because it is the truth, or to do right because it is right. With the opening of Congress, by virtue of the election of Taylor, the Whigs obtained the ascendency in the control of governmental machin-ery. He attended to the duties of the Congres-sional office diligently and with becoming modesty. He answered the letters of his constituents, sent them their public documents, and looked after their pension claims. His only public act of any moment was a bill looking to the emancipation of the slaves in the District of Columbia. He inter-ested Joshua R. Giddings and others of equally as pronounced anti-slavery views in the subject, but his bill eventually found a lodgment on "the table," where it was carefully but promptly laid by a vote of the House.

Meanwhile, being chargeable with the distribu-tion of official patronage, he began to flounder about in explanation of his action in a sea of seem-ingly endless perplexities. His recommendation of the appointment of T. R. King to be Regis-ter or Receiver of the Land Office had pro-duced no little discord among the other aspirants for the place. He wrote to a friend who endorsed and urged the appointment, "either to admit it is wrong, or come forward and sustain him." He then transmits to this same friend a scrap of paper—probably a few lines approving the selection of King—which is to be copied in the friend's own handwriting. "Get everybody," he insists, "(not three or four, but three or four hundred) to sign it, and then send to me. Also have six, eight, or ten of our best known Whig friends to write me additional letters, stating the truth in this matter as they understood it. Don't neglect or delay in the matter. I understand," he continues, "information of an indictment having been found against him three years ago for gaming or keeping a gaming house has been sent to the Department." He then closes with the comforting assurance: "I shall try to take care of it at the Department till your action can be had and forwarded on." And still people insist that Mr. Lincoln was such a guileless man and so free from the politician's sagacity!

In June I wrote him regarding the case of one Walter Davis, who was soured and disappointed because Lincoln had overlooked him in his recommendation for the Springfield post-office. "There must be some mistake," he responds on the 5th, "about Walter Davis saying I promised him the post-office. I did not so promise him. I did tell him that if the distribution of the offices should fall into my hands he should have something; and if I shall be convinced he has said any more than this I shall be disappointed. I said this much to him because, as I understand, he is of good character, is one of the young men, is of the mechanics, is always faithful and never troublesome, a Whig, and is poor, with the support of a widow-mother thrown almost exclusively on him by the death of his brother. If these are wrong reasons then I have been wrong; but I have certainly not been selfish in it, because in my greatest need of friends he was against me and for Baker."

Judge Logan's defeat in 1848 left Lincoln still in a measure in charge of the patronage in his district. After his term in Congress expired the "wriggle and struggle" for office continued; and he was often appealed to for his influence in obtaining, as he termed it, "a way to live without work." Occasionally, when hard pressed, he retorted with bitter sarcasm. I append a letter written in this vein to a gentleman still living in central Illinois, who, I suppose, would prefer that his name should be withheld:

"SPRINGFIELD, Dec. 15, 1849.
"————Esq.
        "DEAR SIR:
    "On my return from Kentucky I found your letter of the 7th of November, and have delayed answering it till now for the reason I now briefly state. From the beginning of our acquaintance I had felt the greatest kindness for you and had supposed it was reciprocated on your part. Last summer, under circumstances which I mentioned to you, I was painfully constrained to withhold a recommendation which you desired, and shortly afterwards I learned, in such a way as to believe it, that you were indulging in open abuse of me. Of course my feelings were wounded. On receiving your last letter the question occurred whether you were attempting to use me at the same time you would

injure me, or whether you might not have been misrepresented to me. If the former, I ought not to answer you; if the latter, I ought, and so I have remained in suspense. I now enclose you the letter, which you may use if you see fit.

"Yours, etc.

"A. LINCOLN."

No doubt the man, when Lincoln declined at first to recommend him, did resort to more or less abuse. That would have been natural, especially with an unsuccessful and disappointed office-seeker. I am inclined to the opinion, and a careful reading of the letter will warrant it, that Lincoln believed him guilty. If the recommendation which Lincoln, after so much reluctance, gave was ever used to further the applicant's cause I do not know it.

With the close of Lincoln's congressional career he drops out of sight as a political factor, and for the next few years we take him up in another capacity. He did not solicit or contend for a renomination to Congress, and such was the unfortunate result of his position on public questions that it is doubtful if he could have succeeded had he done so.

CHAPTER X.

AFTER the wedding of Lincoln and Miss Todd at the Edwards mansion we hear but little of them as a married couple till the spring of 1843, when the husband writes to his friend Speed, who had been joined to his "black-eyed Fanny" a little over a year, with regard to his life as a married man. "Are you possessing houses and lands," he writes, "and oxen and asses and men-servants and maid-servants, and begetting sons and daughters? We are not keeping house, but boarding at the Globe Tavern, which is very well kept now by a widow lady of the name of Beck. Our room (the same Dr. Wallace occupied there) and boarding only costs us four dollars a week." Gaining a livelihood was slow and discouraging business with him, for we find him in another letter apologizing for his failure to visit Kentucky, "because," he says, "I am so poor and make so little headway in the world that I drop back in a month of idleness as much as I gain in a year's sowing." But by dint of untiring efforts and the recognition of influential friends he managed through rare frugality to move along. In his struggles, both in the law and for political advancement, his wife shared in his sacrifices. She was a plucky little woman, and in fact endowed with a more restless ambition than he. She was gifted with a rare insight into the motives that actuate mankind, and there is no doubt that much of Lincoln's success was in a measure attributable to her acuteness and the stimulus of her influence. His election to Congress within four years after their marriage afforded her extreme gratification. She loved power and prominence, and when occasionally she came down to our office, it seemed to me then that she was inordinately proud of her tall and ungainly husband. She saw in him bright prospects ahead, and his every move was watched by her with the closest interest. If to other persons he seemed homely, to her he was the embodiment of noble manhood, and each succeeding day impressed upon her the wisdom of her choice of Lincoln over Douglas—if in reality she ever seriously accepted the latter's attentions. "Mr. Lincoln may not be as handsome a figure," she said one day in the office during her husband's absence, when the conversation turned on Douglas, "but the people are perhaps not aware that his heart is as large as his arms are long."

Mrs. Lincoln accompanied her husband to Washington and remained during one session of Congress. While there they boarded at the same house with Joshua R. Giddings, and when in 1856 the valiant old Abolitionist came to take part in the canvass in Illinois, he early sought out Lincoln, with whom he had been so favorably impressed several years before. On his way home from Congress Lincoln came by way of Niagara Falls and down Lake Erie to Toledo or Detroit. It happened that, some time after, I went to New York and also returned by way of Niagara Falls. In the office, a few days after my return, I was endeavoring to entertain my partner with an account of my trip, and among other things described the Falls. In the attempt I indulged in a good deal of imagery. As I warmed up with the subject my descriptive powers expanded accordingly. The mad rush of water, the roar, the rapids, and the rainbow furnished me with an abundance of material for a stirring and impressive picture. The recollection of the gigantic and awe-inspiring scene stimulated my exuberant powers to the highest pitch. After well-nigh exhausting myself in the effort I turned to Lincoln for his opinion. "What," I inquired, "made the deepest impression on you when you stood in the presence of the great natural wonder? I shall never forget his answer, because it in a very characteristic way illustrates how he looked at everything. "The thing that struck me most forcibly when I saw the Falls," he responded, "was, where in the world did all that water come from?" He had no eye for the magnificence and grandeur of the scene, for the rapids, the mist, the angry waters, and the roar of the whirlpool, but his mind, working in its accustomed channel, heedless of beauty or awe, followed irresistibly back to the first cause. It was in this light he viewed every question. However great the verbal foliage that concealed the nakedness of a good idea Lincoln stripped it all down till he could see clear the way between cause and effect. If there was any secret in his power this surely was it.

After seeing Niagara Falls he continued his journey homeward. At some point on the way, the
vessel on which he had taken passage stranded
on a sand bar. The captain ordered the hands to
collect all the loose planks, empty barrels and boxes
and force them under the sides of the boat. These
empty casks were used to buoy it up. After for-
cing enough of them under the vessel she lifted
gradually and at last swung clear of the opposing
sand bar. Lincoln had watched this operation very
intently. It no doubt carried him back to the
days of his navigation on the turbulent Sangamon,
when he and John Hanks had rendered similar service at New Salem dam to their employer, the
volatile Offut. Continual thinking on the subject
of lifting vessels over sand bars and other obstruc-
tions in the water suggested to him the idea of
inventing an apparatus for the purpose. Using
the principle involved in the operation he had just
witnessed, his plan was to attach a kind of bellows
on each side of the hull of the craft just below the
water line, and, by an odd system of ropes and pulleys, whenever the keel grated on the sand these
bellows were to be filled with air, and thus buoyed
up, the vessel was expected to float clear of the
shoal. On reaching home he at once set to work
to demonstrate the feasibility of his plan. Walter
Davis, a mechanic having a shop near our office,
granted him the use of this tools, and likewise assisted
him in making the model of a miniature vessel with
the arrangement as above described. Lincoln manifested ardent interest in it. Occasionally he would

bring the model in the office, and while whittling on
it would descant on its merits and the revolution
it was destined to work in steamboat navigation.
Although I regarded the thing as impracticable I
said nothing, probably out of respect for Lincoln's
well-known reputation as a boatman. The model
was sent or taken by him to Washington, where a
patent was issued, but the invention was never
applied to any vessel, so far as I ever learned, and
the threatened revolution in steamboat architecture
and navigation never came to pass. The model
still reposes in undisturbed slumber on the shelves
in the Patent Office, and is the only evidence now
existing of Lincoln's success as an inventor.*

Shortly before the close of his term in Congress
he appears in a new rôle. Having failed of a re-
election he became an applicant for the office of
Commissioner of the General Land Office. He had
been urged to this step by many of his Whig friends
in Illinois, but he was so hedged about with other

---

* Following is a copy of Lincoln's application for the patent
on his "Improved Method of Lifting Vessels Over Shoals":
"What I claim as my invention, and desire to secure by letters
patent, is the combination of expansible buoyant chambers
placed at the sides of a vessel with the main shaft or shafts by
means of the sliding spars, which pass down through the buoyant chambers and are made fast to their bottoms and the series
of ropes and pulleys or their equivalents in such a manner that
by turning the main shaft or shafts in one direction the buoyant chambers will be forced downwards into the water, and at
the same time expanded and filled with air for buoying up the
vessel by the displacement of water, and by turning the shafts
in an opposite direction the buoyant chambers will be contracted
into a small space and secured against injury.
                                                "A. LINCOLN."

aspirants from his own State that he soon lost all
heart in the contest. He was too scrupulous, and
lacked too much the essentials of self-confidence and
persistence, to be a successful suitor for office. In a
letter to Joshua Speed, who had written him of a
favorable reference to him by Mr. Crittenden, of
Kentucky,* he says, February 20, 1849, "I am
flattered to learn that Mr. Crittenden has any recollection of me which is not unfavorable; and for the
manifestation of your kindness towards me I sincerely thank you. Still, there is nothing about me
to authorize me to think of a first-class office, and a
second-class one would not compensate me for being
sneered at by others who want it for themselves. I
believe that, so far as the Whigs in Congress are
concerned, I could have the General Land Office
almost by common consent; but then Sweet and
Dav. Morrison and Browning and Cyrus Edwards
all want it, and what is worse, while I think I could
easily take it myself I fear I shall have trouble to
get it for any other man in Illinois. The reason is
that McGaughey, an Indiana ex-member of Congress,
is here after it, and being personally known he will
be hard to beat by any one who is not." But, as
the sequel proved, there was no need to fear the

---

* Lincoln had asked Speed to see Crittenden (then Governor
of Kentucky) and secure from the latter a recommendation for
Baker, who wanted a first-class foreign mission. Crittenden did
not approve of Baker, but suggested that he would favor Lincoln, whom he regarded as a rising man. Speed suggested to
Lincoln to apply for the place himself. "I have pledged myself
to Baker," he answered, "and cannot under any circumstances
consent to the use of my name so long as he is urged for the
same place."

Hoosier stateman, for although he had the endorsement of General Scott and others of equal influence, yet he was left far behind in the race, and along with him Lincoln, Morrison, Browning, and Edwards. A dark horse in the person of Justin Butterfield sprang into view, and with surprising facility captured the tempting prize. This latter and successful aspirant was a lawyer of rather extensive practice and reputation in Chicago. He was shrewd, adroit, and gifted with a knowledge of what politicians would call good management—a quality or characteristic in which Lincoln was strikingly deficient. He had endorsed the Mexican war, but, strangely enough, had lost none of his prestige with the Whigs on that account.*

The close of Congress and the inauguration of Taylor were the signal for Lincoln's departure from Washington. He left with the comforting assur-

---

* The following letter by Butterfield's daughter is not without interest:

CHICAGO, Oct. 12th, 1888.

"MR. JESSE W. WEIK,
  "*Dear Sir:*

"My father was born in Keene, N. H., in 1790, entered Williams College, 1807, and removed to Chicago in 1835. After the re-accession of the Whigs to power he was on the 21st of June in 1849 appointed Commissioner of the Land Office by President Taylor. A competitor for the position at that time was Abraham Lincoln, who was beaten, it was said, by 'the superior dispatch of Butterfield in reaching Washington by the Northern route,' but more correctly by the paramount influence of his friend Daniel Webster.

"He held the position of Land Commissioner until disabled by paralysis in 1852. After lingering for three years in a disabled and enfeebled condition, he died at his home in Chicago, October 23d, 1855, in his sixty-third year.

"Very respectfully,

"ELIZABETH SAWYER."

ance that as an office-seeker he was by no means a
success. Besides his lack of persistence, he had an
unconscious feeling of superiority and pride that
admitted of no such flexibility of opinion as the
professional suitor for office must have, in order to
succeed. He remained but a few days at his home
in Illinois, however, before he again set out for
Washington. The administration of President
Taylor feeling that some reward was due Lincoln
for his heroic efforts on the stump and elsewhere
in behalf of the Whig party and its measures, had
offered him the office of either Governor or Secretary of Oregon, and with the view of considering
this and other offers he returned to Washington.
Lincoln used to relate of this last-named journey
an amusing incident illustrating Kentucky hospitality. He set out from Ransdell's tavern in
Springfield, early in the morning. The only other
passenger in the stage for a good portion of the
distance was a Kentuckian, on his way home from
Missouri. The latter, painfully impressed no doubt
with Lincoln's gravity and melancholy, undertook
to relieve the general monotony of the ride by
offering him a chew of tobacco. With a plain "No,
sir, thank you; I never chew," Lincoln declined,
and a long period of silence followed. Later in
the day the stranger, pulling from his pocket a
leather-covered case, offered Lincoln a cigar, which
he also politely declined on the ground that he
never smoked. Finally, as they neared the station
where horses were to be changed, the Kentuckian,
pouring out a cup of brandy from a flask which had

lain concealed in his satchel, offered it to Lincoln with the remark, "Well, stranger, seeing you don't smoke or chew, perhaps you'll take a little of this French brandy. It's a prime article and a good appetizer besides." His tall and uncommunicative companion declined this last and best evidence of Kentucky hospitality on the same ground as the tobacco. When they separated that afternoon, the Kentuckian, transferring to another stage, bound for Louisville, shook Lincoln warmly by the hand. "See here, stranger," he said, good-humoredly, "you're a clever, but strange companion. I may never see you again, and I don't want to offend you, but I want to say this: my experience has taught me that a man who has no vices has d——d few virtues. Good-day." Lincoln enjoyed this reminiscence of the journey, and took great pleasure in relating it. During this same journey occurred an incident for which Thomas H. Nelson, of Terre Haute, Indiana, who was appointed Minister to Chili by Lincoln, when he was President, is authority. "In the spring of 1849," relates Nelson, "Judge Abram Hammond, who was afterwards Governor of Indiana, and I arranged to go from Terre Haute to Indianapolis in the stage coach. An entire day was usually consumed in the journey. By daybreak the stage had arrived from the West, and as we stepped in we discovered that the entire back seat was occupied by a long, lank individual, whose head seemed to protrude from one end of the coach and his feet from the other. He was the sole occupant, and was sleeping soundly. Hammond slapped him familiarly on the shoulder, and asked him if he had chartered the stage for the day. The stranger, now wide awake, responded, 'Certainly not,' and at once took the front seat, politely surrendering to us the place of honor and comfort. We took in our travelling companion at a glance. A queer, odd-looking fellow he was, dressed in a well-worn and ill-fitting suit of bombazine, without vest or cravat, and a twenty-five-cent palm hat on the back of his head. His very prominent features in repose seemed dull and expressionless. Regarding him as a good subject for merriment we perpetrated several jokes. He took them all with the utmost innocence and good-nature, and joined in the laugh, although at his own expense. At noon we stopped at a wayside hostelry for dinner. We invited him to eat with us, and he approached the table as if he considered it a great honor. He sat with about half his person on a small chair, and held his hat under his arm during the meal. Resuming our journey after dinner, conversation drifted into a discussion of the comet, a subject that was then agitating the scientific world, in which the stranger took the deepest interest. He made many · startling suggestions and asked many questions. We amazed him with words of learned length and thundering sound. After an astounding display of wordy pyrotechnics the dazed and bewildered stranger asked: 'What is going to be the upshot of this comet business?' I replied that I was not certain, in fact I differed from most scien-

tists and philosophers, and was inclined to the
opinion that the world would follow the darned
thing off! Late in the evening we reached Indianapolis, and hurried to Browning's hotel, losing
sight of the stranger altogether. We retired to
our room to brush and wash away the dust of the
journey. In a few minutes I descended to the
portico, and there descried our long, gloomy fellow-
traveller in the center of an admiring group of
lawyers, among whom were Judges McLean and
Huntington, Edward Hannigan, Albert S. White,
and Richard W. Thompson, who seemed to be
amused and interested in a story he was telling.
I enquired of Browning, the landlord, who he was.
"Abraham Lincoln, of Illinois, a member of Congress," was the response. I was thunderstruck at
the announcement. I hastened upstairs and told
Hammond the startling news, and together we
emerged from the hotel by a back door and went
down an alley to another house, thus avoiding further contact with our now distinguished fellow-
traveller. Curiously enough, years after this, Hammond had vacated the office of Governor of Indiana a few days before Lincoln arrived in Indianapolis, on his way to Washington to be inaugurated
President. I had many opportunities after the
stage ride to cultivate Mr. Lincoln's acquaintance,
and was a zealous advocate of his nomination and
election to the Presidency. Before leaving his
home for Washington, Mr. Lincoln caused John P.
Usher and myself to be invited to accompany him.
We agreed to join him in Indianapolis. On reach-

ing that city the Presidential party had already
arrived, and upon inquiry we were informed that
the President-elect was in the dining-room of the
hotel, at supper. Passing through, we saw that
every seat at the numerous tables was occupied,
but failed to find Mr. Lincoln. As we were nearing the door to the office of the hotel, a long arm
reached to my shoulder and a shrill voice exclaimed, 'Hello, Nelson! do you think, after all,
the world is going to follow the darned thing off?'
It was Mr. Lincoln."

The benefits and advantages of the territorial
posts offered by President Taylor to Lincoln were
freely discussed by the latter's friends. Some urged
his acceptance on the usual ground that when Oregon was admitted as a State, he might be its first
Senator. Lincoln himself had some inclination to
accept. He told me himself that he felt by his
course in Congress he had committed political suicide, and wanted to try a change of locality—hence
the temptation to go to Oregon. But when he
brought the proposition home to his fireside, his
wife put her foot squarely down on it with a firm
and emphatic No. That always ended it with
Lincoln. The result of the whole thing proved
a fortunate deliverance for him, the propriety of
which became more apparent as the years rolled
by.*

---

* About this time Grant Goodrich, a lawyer in Chicago, proposed to take Lincoln into partnership with him. Goodrich had
an extensive and paying practice there, but Lincoln refused the
offer, giving as a reason that he tended to consumption, and, if

While a member of Congress and otherwise immersed in politics Lincoln seemed to lose all interest in the law. Of course, what practice he himself controlled passed into other hands. I retained all the business I could, and worked steadily on until, when he returned, our practice was as extensive as that of any other firm at the bar. Lincoln realized that much of this was due to my efforts, and on his return he therefore suggested that he had no right to share in the business and profits which I had made. I responded that, as he had aided me and given me prominence when I was young and needed it, I could afford now to be grateful if not generous. I therefore recommended a continuation of the partnership, and we went on as before. I could notice a difference in Lincoln's movement as a lawyer from this time forward. He had begun to realize a certain lack of discipline—a want of mental training and method. Ten years had wrought some change in the law, and more in the lawyers, of Illinois. The conviction had settled in the minds of the people that the pyrotechnics of court room and stump oratory did not necessarily imply extensive or profound ability in the lawyer who resorted to it. The courts were becoming graver and more learned, and the lawyer was learning as a preliminary and indispensable condition to

---

he removed to a city like Chicago, he would have to sit down and study harder than ever. The close application required of him and the confinement in the office, he contended, would soon kill him. He preferred going around on the circuit, and even if he earned smaller fees he felt much happier.

success that he must be a close reasoner, besides having at command a broad knowledge of the principles on which the statutory law is constructed. There was of course the same riding on circuit as before, but the courts had improved in tone and morals, and there was less laxity—at least it appeared so to Lincoln. Political defeat had wrought a marked effect on him. It went below the skin and made a changed man of him. He was not soured at his seeming political decline, but still he determined to eschew politics from that time forward and devote himself entirely to the law. And now he began to make up for time lost in politics by studying the law in earnest. No man had greater power of application than he. Once fixing his mind on any subject, nothing could interfere with or disturb him. Frequently I would go out on the circuit with him. We, usually, at the little country inns occupied the same bed. In most cases the beds were too short for him, and his feet would hang over the floor-board, thus exposing a limited expanse of shin bone. Placing a candle on a chair at the head of the bed, he would read and study for hours. I have known him to study in this position till two o'clock in the morning. Meanwhile, I and others who chanced to occupy the same room would be safely and soundly asleep. On the circuit in this way he studied Euclid until he could with ease demonstrate all the propositions in the six books. How he could maintain his mental equilibrium or concentrate his thoughts on an abstract mathematical proposition,

while Davis, Logan, Swett, Edwards, and I so in-
dustriously and volubly filled the air with our
interminable snoring was a problem none of us
could ever solve. I was on the circuit with Lincoln probably one-fourth of the time. The remainder of my time was spent in Springfield looking
after the business there, but I know that life on the
circuit was a gay one. It was rich with incidents,
and afforded the nomadic lawyers ample relaxation
from all the irksome toil that fell to their lot.
Lincoln loved it. I suppose it would be a fair
estimate to state that he spent over half the year
following Judges Treat and Davis around on the
circuit. On Saturdays the court and attorneys, if
within a reasonable distance, would usually start
for their homes. Some went for a fresh supply of
clothing, but the greater number went simply to
spend a day of rest with their families. The only
exception was Lincoln, who usually spent his Sun-
days with the loungers at the country tavern, and
only went home at the end of the circuit or term of
court. "At first," * relates one of his colleagues
on the circuit, "we wondered at it, but soon learned
to account for his strange disinclination to go
home. Lincoln himself never had much to say
about home, and we never felt free to comment on
it. Most of us had pleasant, inviting homes, and as
we struck out for them I'm sure each one of us down
in our hearts had a mingled feeling of pity and sympathy for him." If the day was long and he was

---

* David Davis, MS.

oppressed, the feeling was soon relieved by the narration of a story. The tavern loungers enjoyed it,
and his melancholy, taking to itself wings, seemed
to fly away. In the role of a story-teller I am
prone to regard Mr. Lincoln as without an equal.
I have seen him surrounded by a crowd numbering
as many as two and in some cases three hundred
persons, all deeply interested in the outcome of a
story which, when he had finished it, speedily
found repetition in every grocery and lounging
place within reach. His power of mimicry, as I
have before noted, and his manner of recital, were
in many respects unique, if not remarkable. His
countenance and all his features seemed to take
part in the performance. As he neared the pith or
point of the joke or story every vestige of serious-
ness disappeared from his face. His little gray
eyes sparkled; a smile seemed to gather up, curtain like, the corners of his mouth; his frame quivered with suppressed excitement; and when the
point—or "nub" of the story, as he called it—came,
no one's laugh was heartier than his. These back-
woods allegories are out of date now, and any
lawyer, ambitious to gain prominence, would hardly
dare thus to entertain a crowd, except at the risk
of his reputation; but with Lincoln it gave him, in
some mysterious way, a singularly firm hold on the
people.

Lincoln was particularly strong in Menard county,
and while on the circuit there he met with William
Engle and James Murray, two men who were
noted also for their story-telling proclivities. I

am not now asserting for the country and the period what would at a later day be considered a very high standard of taste. Art had not such patrons as to-day, but the people loved the beautiful as Nature furnished it, and the good as they found it, with as much devotion as the more refined classes now are joined to their idols. Newspapers were scarce, and the court-house, with its cluster of itinerant lawyers, disseminated much of the information that was afterwards broken up into smaller bits at the pioneer's fireside. A curious civilization indeed, but one through which every Western State distant from the great arterial river or seaboard has had to pass.

When Lincoln, Murray, and Engle met, there was sure to be a crowd. All were more or less masters in their art. I have seen the little country tavern where these three were wont to meet after an adjournment of court, crowded almost to suffocation with an audience of men who had gathered to witness the contest among the members of the strange triumvirate. The physician of the town, all the lawyers, and not unfrequently a preacher could be found in the crowd that filled the doors and windows. The yarns they spun and the stories they told would not bear repetition here, but many of them had morals which, while exposing the weaknesses of mankind, stung like a whip-lash. Some were no doubt a thousand years old, with just enough "verbal varnish" and alterations of names and dates to make them new and crisp. By virtue of the last-named application, Lincoln was enabled to draw from Balzac a "droll story," and locating it in "Egypt"* or in Indiana, pass it off for a purely original conception. Every recital was followed by its "storm of laughter and chorus of cheers." After this had all died down, some unfortunate creature, through whose thickened skull the point had just penetrated, would break out in a guffaw, starting another wave of laughter which, growing to the proportions of a billow, would come rolling in like a veritable breaker. I have known these story-telling jousts to continue long after midnight—in some cases till the very small hours of the morning. I have seen Judge Treat, who was the very impersonation of gravity itself, sit up till the last and laugh until, as he often expressed it, "he almost shook his ribs loose." The next day he would ascend the bench and listen to Lincoln in a murder trial, with all the seeming severity of an English judge in wig and gown. Amid such surroundings, a leading figure in such society, alternately reciting the latest effusion of the bar-room or mimicking the clownish antics of the negro minstrel, he who was destined to be an immortal emancipator, was steadily and unconsciously nearing the great trial of his life. We shall see further on how this rude civilization crystallized both his logic and his wit for use in another day.

Reverting again to Mr. Lincoln as a lawyer, it is proper to add that he detested the mechanical work of the office. He wrote few papers—less perhaps than any other man at the bar. Such work was

---

* The word Egypt, so frequently used in this book, refers to that portion of Illinois which lies south of the famous National Road.

usually left to me for the first few years we were together. Afterwards we made good use of students who came to learn the law in our office. A Chicago lawyer,* in a letter to me about Mr. Lincoln, in 1866, says: "Lincoln once told me that he had taken you in as a partner, supposing you had system and would keep things in order, but that he found out you had no more system than he had, but that you were in reality a good lawyer, so that he was doubly disappointed." Lincoln knew no such thing as order or method in his law practice. He made no preparation in advance, but trusted to the hour for its inspiration and to Providence for his supplies. In the matter of letter-writing† he made no distinction between one of a business nature or any other kind. If a happy thought or expression struck him he was by no means reluctant to use it. As early as 1839 he wrote to a gentle-

---

* W. C. Whitney, MS.

† "I wish you would learn of Everett what he would take, over and above a discharge, for all trouble we have been at to take his business out of our hands and give it to somebody else. It is impossible to collect money on that or any other claim here, now, and although you know I am not a very petulant man, I declare that I am almost out of patience with Mr. Everett's endless importunities. It seems like he not only writes all the letters he can himself, but he gets everybody else in Louisville and vicinity to be constantly writing to us about his claim. I have always said that Mr. Everett is a very clever fellow, and I am very sorry he cannot be obliged; but it does seem to me he ought to know we are interested to collect his claim, and therefore would do it if we could. I am neither joking nor in a pet when I say we would thank him to transfer his business to some other, without any compensation for what we have done, provided he will see the court costs paid for which we are security."—MS. letter to Joshua F. Speed, March 27, 1842.

man about a matter of business, observing crustily
that "a d——d hawk-billed Yankee is here besetting
me at every turn I take, saying that Robert Kenzie
never received the $80 to which he was entitled."
In July, 1851, he wrote a facetious message to one of
his clients, saying: "I have news from Ottawa that
we win our case. As the Dutch justice said when
he married folks, 'Now where ish my hundred tol-
lars.' "* He was proverbially careless as to habits.
In a letter to a fellow-lawyer in another town, apologizing for failure to answer sooner, he explains:
"First, I have been very busy in the United States
Court; second, when I received the letter I put it
in my old hat and buying a new one the next day
the old one was set aside, and so the letter was lost
sight of for a time." This hat of Lincoln's—a silk
plug—was an extraordinary receptacle. It was his
desk and his memorandum-book. In it he carried

---

* The following unpublished letter in possession of C. F. Gun-
ther, Esq., Chicago, Ills., shows how he proposed to fill a vacancy in the office of Clerk of the United States Court. It reads
like the letter of a politician in the midst of a canvass for office:

"SPRINGFIELD, ILL., December 6, 1854.
"Hon. JUSTICE MCLEAN.

"SIR: I understand it is in contemplation to displace the
present Clerk and appoint a new one for the Circuit and District
Courts of Illinois. I am very friendly to the present incum-
bent, and both for his own sake and that of his family, I wish
him to be retained so long as it is possible for the Court to do so.

"In the contingency of his removal, however, I have recommended William Butler as his successor, and I do not wish what
I write now to be taken as any abatement of that recommendation.

"William J. Black is also an applicant for the appointment,
and I write this at the solicitation of his friends to say that he
is every way worthy of the office, and that I doubt not the
conferring it upon him will give great satisfaction.
"Your ob't servant,
"A. LINCOLN."

his bank book and the bulk of his letters. Whenever in his reading or researches he wished to preserve an idea, he jotted it down on an envelope or stray piece of paper and placed it inside the lining. Afterwards when the memorandum was needed there was only one place to look for it.*

How Lincoln appeared and acted in the law office has been graphically and, I must confess, truthfully told by a gentleman now in New York, who was for several years a student in our office. I beg to quote a few lines from him: "My brother met Mr. Lincoln in Ottawa, Ill.,† one day, and said to him: 'I have a brother whom I would very much like to have enter your office as a student.' 'All right!' was his reply; 'send him down and we will take a look at him.' I was then studying law at Grand Rapids, Mich., and on hearing from my brother I immediately packed up and started for Springfield. I arrived there on Saturday night. On Sunday Mr. Lincoln was pointed out to me. I well remember this first sight of him. He was striding along, holding little Tad, then about six years old, by the hand, who could with the greatest difficulty keep up with his father. In the morning I applied at the office of

---

* Lincoln had always on the top of our desk a bundle of papers into which he slipped anything he wished to keep and afterwards refer to. It was a receptacle of general information. Some years ago, on removing the furniture from the office, I took down the bundle and blew from the top the liberal coat of dust that had accumulated thereon. Immediately underneath the string was a slip bearing this endorsement, in his hand: "When you can't find it anywhere else, look in this."

† John H. Littlefield. *Brooklyn Eagle*, October 16, 1887.

Lincoln and Herndon for admission as a student.
The office was on the second floor of a brick building
on the public square, opposite the court-house.
You went up one flight of stairs and then passed
along a hallway to the rear office, which was a
medium-sized room. There was one long table in
the center of the room, and a shorter one running
in the opposite direction, forming a T, and both
were covered with green baize. There were two
windows which looked into the back yard. In one
corner was an old-fashioned secretary with pigeon-
holes and a drawer, and here Mr. Lincoln and his
partner kept their law papers. There was also a
book-case containing about 200 volumes of law as
well as miscellaneous books. The morning I entered the office Mr. Lincoln and his partner, Mr.
Herndon, were both present. Mr. Lincoln addressed
his partner thus: 'Billy, this is the young man of
whom I spoke to you. Whatever arrangement you
make with him will be satisfactory to me.' Then,
turning to me, he said, 'I hope you will not become
so enthusiastic in your studies of Blackstone and
Kent as did two young men whom we had here.
Do you see that spot over there?' pointing to a
large ink stain on the wall. 'Well, one of these
young men got so enthusiastic in his pursuit of legal
lore that he fired an inkstand at the other one's
head, and that is the mark he made.' I immediately
began to clean up about the office a little. Mr.
Lincoln had been in Congress and had the usual
amount of seeds to distribute to the farmers. These
were sent out with Free Soil and Republican docu-

ments. In my efforts to clean up, I found that some of the seeds had sprouted in the dirt that had collected in the office. Judge Logan and Milton Hay occupied the front offices on the same floor with Lincoln and Herndon, and one day Mr. Hay came in and said with apparent astonishment: 'What's happened here?' 'Oh, nothing,' replied Lincoln, pointing to me, 'only this young man has been cleaning up a little.' One of Lincoln's striking characteristics was his simplicity, and nowhere was this trait more strikingly exhibited than in his willingness to receive instruction from anybody and everybody. One day he came into the office and addressing his partner, said: 'Billy, what's the meaning of antithesis?' Mr. Herndon gave him the definition of the word, and I said: 'Mr. Lincoln, if you will allow me, I will give you an example.' 'All right, John, go ahead,' said Mr. Lincoln in his hearty manner. 'Phillips says, in his essay on Napoleon, "A pretended patriot, he impoverished the country; a professed Catholic, he imprisoned the Pope,"' etc. Mr. Lincoln thanked me and seemed very much pleased. Returning from off the circuit once he said to Mr. Herndon: 'Billy, I heard a good story while I was up in the country. Judge D—— was complimenting the landlord on the excellence of his beef. "I am surprised," he said, "that you have such good beef. You must have to kill a whole critter when you want any." "Yes," said the landlord, "we never kill less than a whole critter."

"Lincoln's favorite position when unravelling some knotty law point was to stretch both of his legs at full length upon a chair in front of him. In this position, with books on the table near by and in his lap, he worked up his case. No matter how deeply interested in his work, if any one came in he had something humorous and pleasant to say, and usually wound up by telling a joke or an anecdote. I have heard him relate the same story three times within as many hours to persons who came in at different periods, and every time he laughed as heartily and enjoyed it as if it were a new story. His humor was infectious. I had to laugh because I thought it funny that Mr. Lincoln enjoyed a story so repeatedly told.

"There was no order in the office at all. The firm of Lincoln and Herndon kept no books. They divided their fees without taking any receipts or making any entries on books. One day Mr. Lincoln received $5,000 as a fee in a railroad case. He came in and said; 'Well, Billy,' addressing his partner, Mr. Herndon, 'here is our fee; sit down and let me divide.' He counted out $2,500 to his partner, and gave it to him with as much nonchalance as he would have given a few cents for a paper. Cupidity had no abiding place in his nature.

"I took a good deal of pains in getting up a speech which I wanted to deliver during a political campaign. I told Mr. Lincoln that I would like to read it to him. He sat down in one chair, put his feet into another one, and said: 'John, you can fire away with that speech; I guess I can stand it.' I unrolled the manuscript, and proceeded with some trepidation. 'That's a good point, John,' he would say, at certain places, and at others: 'That's good —very good indeed,' until I felt very much elated over my effort. I delivered the speech over fifty times during the campaign. Elmer E. Ellsworth, afterwards colonel of the famous Zouaves, who was killed in Alexandria, early in the war, was nominally a student in Lincoln's office. His head was so full of military matters, however, that he thought little of law. Of Ellsworth, Lincoln said: 'That young man has a real genius for war!' "

During the six years following his retirement from Congress, Lincoln, realizing in a marked degree his want of literary knowledge, extended somewhat his research in that direction. He was naturally indisposed to undertake anything that savored of exertion, but his brief public career had exposed the limited area of his literary attainments. Along with his Euclid therefore he carried a well-worn copy of Shakespeare, in which he read no little in his leisure moments. "In travelling on the circuit," relates one of his associates at the bar,* "he was in the habit of rising earlier than his brothers of the bar. On such occasions he was wont to sit by the fire, having uncovered the coals, and muse, and ponder, and soliloquize, inspired, no doubt, by that strange psychological influence which is so poetically described by Poe in 'The Raven.' On one of these occasions, at the town of Lincoln, sitting in the position described, he quoted aloud and at length the poem called 'Immortality.' When he

---

* Lawrence Weldon, letter, Feb. 10, 1866, MS.

had finished he was questioned as to the authorship and where it could be found. He had forgotten the author, but said that to him it sounded as much like true poetry as anything he had ever heard. He was particularly pleased with the last two stanzas."

Beyond a limited acquaintance with Shakespeare, Byron, and Burns, Mr. Lincoln, comparatively speaking, had no knowledge of literature. He was familiar with the Bible, and now and then evinced a fancy for some poem or short sketch to which his attention was called by some one else, or which he happened to run across in his cursory reading of books or newspapers. He never in his life sat down and read a book through, and yet he could readily quote any number of passages from the few volumes whose pages he had hastily scanned. In addition to his well-known love for the poem "Immortality" or "Why should the Spirit of Mortal be Proud," he always had a great fondness for Oliver Wendell Holmes' "Last Leaf," the fourth stanza of which, beginning with the verse, "The mossy marbles rest," I have often heard him repeat. He once told me of a song a young lady had sung in his hearing at a time when he was laboring under some dejection of spirits. The lines struck his fancy, and although he did not know the singer—having heard her from the sidewalk as he passed her house—he sent her a request to write the lines out for him. Within a day or two he came into the office, carrying in his hand a delicately perfumed envelope which bore the address, "Mr. Lincoln—

Present," in an unmistakable female hand. In it, written on gilt-edged paper, were the lines of the song. The plaintive strain of the piece and its melancholy sentiment struck a responsive chord in a heart already filled with gloom and sorrow. Though ill-adapted to dissipate one's depression, something about it charmed Lincoln, and he read and re-read it with increasing relish. I had forgotten the circumstance until recently, when, in going over some old papers and letters turned over to me by Mr. Lincoln, I ran across the manuscript, and the incident was brought vividly to my mind. The envelope, still retaining a faint reminder of the perfumed scent given it thirty years before, bore the laconic endorsement, "poem—I like this," in the handwriting of Mr. Lincoln. Unfortunately no name accompanied the manuscript, and unless the lady on seeing this chooses to make herself known, we shall probably not learn who the singer was. The composition is headed, "The Enquiry." I leave it to my musical friends to render it into song. Following are the lines:

"Tell me, ye winged winds
That round my pathway roar,
Do ye not know some spot
Where mortals weep no more?
Some lone and pleasant vale
Some valley in the West,
Where, free from toil and pain,
The weary soul may rest?
The loud wind dwindled to a whisper low,
And sighed for pity as it answered, No.

"Tell me, thou mighty deep,
Whose billows round me play,
Know'st thou some favored spot,
Some island far away,
Where weary man may find
The bliss for which he sighs;
Where sorrow never lives
And friendship never dies?
The loud waves rolling in perpetual flow
Stopped for awhile and sighed to answer, No.

"And thou, serenest moon,
That with such holy face
Dost look upon the Earth
Asleep in Night's embrace—
Tell me, in all thy round
Hast thou not seen some spot
Where miserable man
Might find a happier lot?
Behind a cloud the moon withdrew in woe,
And a voice sweet but sad responded, No.

"Tell me, my secret soul,
Oh, tell me, Hope and Faith,
Is there no resting-place
From sorrow, sin, and death?
Is there no happy spot
Where mortals may be blessed,
Where grief may find a balm
And weariness a rest?
Faith, Hope, and Love, best boon to mortals given,
Waved their bright wings and whispered, Yes, in Heaven."*

Judge S. H. Treat, recently deceased, thus

---

* Persons familiar with literature will recognize this as a
poem written by Charles Mackay, an English writer who represented a London newspaper in the United States during the
Rebellion as its war correspondent. It was set to music as a
chant, and as such was frequently rendered in public by the
famous Hutchinson family of singers. I doubt if Mr. Lincoln
ever knew who wrote it.

describes Lincoln's first appearance in the Supreme Court of Illinois. "A case being called for hearing, Mr. Lincoln stated that he appeared for the appellant and was ready to proceed with the argument. He then said: 'This is the first case I have ever had in this court, and I have therefore examined it with great care. As the Court will perceive by looking at the abstract of the record, the only question in the case is one of authority. I have not been able to 'find any authority to sustain my side of the case, but I have found several cases directly in point on the other side. I will now give these authorities to the court, and then submit the case."

A lawyer in Beardstown relates this:* "Lincoln came into my office one day with the remark: 'I see you've been suing some of my clients, and I've come down to see about it.' He had reference to a suit I had brought to enforce the specific performance of a contract. I explained the case to him, and showed my proofs. He seemed surprised that I should deal so frankly with him, and said he would be as frank with me; that my client was justly entitled to a decree, and he should so represent it to the court; and that it was against his principles to contest a clear matter of right. So my client got a deed for a farm which, had another lawyer been in Mr. Lincoln's place, would have been consumed by the costs of litigation for years, with the result probably the same in the end." A young man once wrote to Lincoln, enquiring for the

* J. Henry Shaw, letter, June 13, 1866, MS.

best mode of obtaining a thorough knowledge of the law. "The mode is very simple," he responded, "though laborious and tedious. It is only to get books and read and study them carefully. Begin with Blackstone's Commentaries, and after reading carefully through, say twice, take up Chitty's Pleadings, Greenleaf's Evidence, and Story's Equity in succession. Work, work, work, is the main thing."*

Lincoln never believed in suing for a fee. If a client would not pay on request he never sought to enforce collection. I remember once a man who had been indicted for forgery or fraud employed us to defend him. The illness of the prosecuting attorney caused some delay in the case, and our client, becoming dissatisfied at our conduct of the case, hired some one else, who superseded us most effectually. The defendant declining to pay us the fee demanded, on the ground that we had not represented him at the trial of the cause, I brought suit against him in Lincoln's absence and obtained judgment for our fee. After Lincoln's return from the circuit the fellow hunted him up and by means of a carefully constructed tale prevailed on him to release the judgment without receiving a cent of pay. The man's unkind treatment of us deserved no such mark of generosity from Lincoln, and yet he could not resist the appeal of any one in poverty and want. He could never turn from a

---

* Letter to J. M. Brockman, Sept. 25, 1859, MS.

woman in tears.* It was no surprise to me or any of his intimate friends that so many designing women with the conventional widows' weeds and easy-flowing tears overcame him in Washington. It was difficult for him to detect an imposter, and hence it is not to be marvelled at that he cautioned his secretaries: "Keep them away—I cannot stand it."

On many questions I used to grow somewhat enthusiastic, adopting sometimes a lofty metaphor by way of embellishment. Lincoln once warned me; "Billy, don't shoot too high—aim lower and the common people will understand you. They are the ones you want to reach—at least they are the ones you ought to reach. The educated and refined people will understand you any way. If you aim too high your ideas will go over the heads of the masses, and only hit those who need no hitting." While it is true that from his peculiar construction Lincoln dwelt entirely in the head and in the land of thought, and while he was physically a lazy man, yet he was intellectually energetic; he was not only energetic, but industrious; not only industrious, but tireless; not only tireless, but indefatigable. Therefore if in debate with him a man stood on a questionable foundation he might well watch whereon he stood. Lincoln could look a long distance ahead and calculate the triumph of right. With him justice and truth were paramount. If to him

---

* I have heard Lincoln say he thanked God that he was not born a woman, because he could not refuse any request if it was not apparently dishonest.

a thing seemed untrue he could not in his nature
simulate truth. His retention by a man to defend
a lawsuit did not prevent him from throwing it up
in its most critical stage if he believed he was
espousing an unjust cause. This extreme conscien-
tiousness and disregard of the alleged sacredness
of the professional cloak robbed him of much so-
called success at the bar. He once wrote to one of
our clients: "I do not think there is the least use
of doing anything more with your lawsuit. I not
only do not think you are sure to gain it, but I do
think you are sure to lose it. Therefore the sooner
it ends the better."* Messrs. Stuart and Edwards
once brought a suit against a client of ours which
involved the title to considerable property. At
that time we had only two or three terms of court,
and the docket was somewhat crowded. The plaintiff's attorneys were pressing us for a trial, and we
were equally as anxious to ward it off. What we
wanted were time and a continuance to the next
term. We dared not make an affidavit for continuance, founded on facts, because no such pertinent
and material facts as the law contemplated existed.
Our case for the time seemed hopeless. One morning, however, I accidentally overheard a remark
from Stuart indicating his fear lest a certain fact
should happen to come into our possession. I felt
some relief, and at once drew up a ficititious plea,
averring as best I could the substance of the
doubts I knew existed in Stuart's mind. The

* Letter to H. Keeling, Esq., March 3, 1858, MS.

plea was as skilfully drawn as I knew how, and was framed as if we had the evidence to sustain it. The whole thing was a sham, but so constructed as to work the desired continuance, because I knew that Stuart and Edwards believed the facts were as I pleaded them. This was done in the absence and without the knowledge of Lincoln. The plea could not be demurred to, and the opposing counsel dared not take the issue on it. It perplexed them sorely. At length, before further steps were taken, Lincoln came into court. He looked carefully over all the papers in the case, as was his custom, and seeing my engenious subterfuge, asked, "Is this seventh plea a good one?" Proud of the exhibition of my skill, I answered that it was. "But," he inquired, incredulously, "is it founded on fact?" I was obliged to respond in the negative, at the same time following up my answer with an explanation of what I had overheard Stuart intimate, and of how these alleged facts could be called facts if a certain construction were put upon them. I insisted that our position was justifiable, and that our client must have time or be ruined. I could see at once it failed to strike Lincoln as just right. He scratched his head thoughtfully and asked, "Hadn't we better withdraw that plea? You know it's a sham, and a sham is very often but another name for a lie. Don't let it go on record. The cursed thing may come staring us in the face long after this suit has been forgotten." The plea was withdrawn. By some agency—not our own—the case was continued and our client's interests were saved.

I only relate this incident to illustrate Lincoln's far-seeing capacity; it serves to show how over-cautious he seemed to be with regard to how his record might look in the future. I venture the assertion that he was the only member of the bar in Springfield who would have taken such a conscientious view of the matter.

One phase of Lincoln's character, almost lost sight of in the commonly accepted belief in his humility and kindly feeling under all circumstances, was his righteous indignation when aroused. In such cases he was the most fearless man I ever knew. I remember a murder case in which we appeared for the defense, and during the trial of which the judge—a man of ability far inferior to Lincoln's—kept ruling against us. Finally, a very material question, in fact one around which the entire case seemed to revolve, came up, and again the Court ruled adversely. The prosecution was jubilant, and Lincoln, seeing defeat certain unless he recovered his ground, grew very despondent. The notion crept into his head that the Court's rulings, which were absurd and almost spiteful, were aimed at him, and this angered him beyond reason. He told me of his feelings at dinner, and said: "I have determined to crowd the Court to the wall and regain my position before night." From that time forward it was interesting to watch him. At the reassembling of court he arose to read a few authorities in support of his position. In his comments he kept within the bounds of propriety just far enough to avoid a reprimand for contempt of court.

He characterized the continued rulings against him as not only unjust but foolish; and, figuratively speaking, he pealed the Court from head to foot. I shall never forget the scene. Lincoln had the crowd, a portion of the bar, and the jury with him. He knew that fact, and it, together with the belief that injustice had been done him, nerved him to a feeling of desperation. He was wrought up to the point of madness. When a man of large heart and head is wrought up and mad, as the old adage runs, "he's mad all over." Lincoln had studied up the points involved, but knowing full well the calibre of the judge, relied mostly on the moral effect of his personal bearing and influence. He was alternately furious and eloquent, pursuing the Court with broad facts and pointed inquiries in marked and rapid succession. I remember he made use of this homely incident in illustration of some point: "In early days a party of men went out hunting for a wild boar. But the game came upon them unawares, and scampering away they all climbed the trees save one, who, seizing the animal by the ears, undertook to hold him, but despairing of success cried out to his companions in the trees, 'For God's sake, boys, come down and help me let go.' " The prosecution endeavored to break him down or even "head him off," but all to no purpose. His masterly arraignment of law and facts had so effectually badgered the judge that, strange as it may seem, he pretended to see the error in his former position, and finally reversed his decision in Lincoln's favor. The latter saw his triumph, and surveyed a situation of which he was the master. His client was acquitted, and he had swept the field.

In the case of Parker *vs.* Hoyt, tried in the United States Court in Chicago, Lincoln was one of the counsel for the defendant. The suit was on the merits of an infringement of a patent water wheel. The trial lasted several days and Lincoln manifested great interest in the case. In his earlier days he had run, or aided in running, a saw-mill, and explained in his argument the action of the water on the wheel in a manner so clear and intelligible that the jury were enabled to comprehend the points and line of defence without the least difficulty. It was evident he had carried the jury with him in a most masterly argument, the force of which could not be broken by the reply of the opposing counsel. After the jury retired he became very anxious and uneasy. The jury were in another building, the windows of which opened on the street, and had been out for some two hours. "In passing along the street, one of the jurors on whom we very much relied," relates Lincoln's associate in the case,* "he being a very intelligent man and firm in his convictions, held up to him one finger. Mr. Lincoln became very much excited, fearing it indicated that eleven of the jury were against him. He knew if this man was for him he would never yield his opinion. He added, if he was like a juryman he had in Tazewell county, the defendant was safe. He was there employed, he said, to prosecute a suit for

---

* Grant Goodrich, letter, Nov. 9, 1866, MS.

divorce. His client was a pretty, refined, and interesting little woman, and in court. The defendant,
her husband, was a gross, morose, querulous, fault-
finding, and uncomfortable man, and entirely unfit-
ted for the husband of such a woman; but although
he was able to prove the use of very offensive and
vulgar epithets applied by the husband to his wife,
and all sorts of annoyances, yet there were no such
acts of personal violence as were required by the
statute to justify a divorce. Lincoln did the best
he could, and appealed to the jury to have compas-
sion on the woman, and not to bind her to such a
man and such a life as awaited her if required to
live longer with him. The jury took about the
same view of it in their deliberations. They desired to find for his fair client, but could discover
no evidence which would really justify a verdict
for her. At last they drew up a verdict for the defendant, and all signed but one fellow, who on being approached with the verdict said, coolly: 'Gentlemen, I am going to lie down to sleep, and when
you get ready to give a verdict for that little
woman, then wake me and not until then; for before I will give a verdict against her I will lie here
till I rot and the pismires carry me out through the
key-hole.' 'Now,' observed Lincoln, 'if that juryman will stick like the man in Tazewell county we
are safe.' Strange to relate, the jury did come in,
and with a verdict for the defendant. Lincoln
always regarded this as one of the gratifying
triumphs of his professional life."

CHAPTER XI.

A LAW office is a dull, dry place so far as pleasurable or interesting incidents are concerned. If one is in search of stories of fraud, deceit, cruelty, broken promises, blasted homes, there is no better place to learn them than a law office. But to the majority of persons these painful recitals are anything but attractive, and it is well perhaps that it should be so. In the office, as in the court room, Lincoln, when discussing any point, was never arbitrary or insinuating. He was deferential, cool, patient, and respectful. When he reached the office, about nine o'clock in the morning, the first thing he did was to pick up a newspaper, spread himself out on an old sofa, one leg on a chair, and read aloud, much to my discomfort. Singularly enough Lincoln never read any other way but aloud. This habit used to annoy me almost beyond the point of endurance. I once asked him why he did so. This was his explanation: "When I read aloud two senses catch the idea: first, I see what I read; second, I hear it, and therefore I can remember it better." He never studied law books unless a case was on hand for consideration—never followed up the decisions of the supreme courts, as other lawyers did. It seemed as if he depended for

his effectiveness in managing a law suit entirely on
the stimulus and inspiration of the final hour. He
paid but little attention to the fees and money matters of the firm—usually leaving all such to me.
He never entered an item in the account book. If
any one paid money to him which belonged to the
firm, on arriving at the office he divided it with me.
If I was not there, he would wrap up my share in a
piece of paper and place it in my drawer—marking
it with a pencil, "Case of Roe *vs.* Doe.—Herndon's
half."

On many topics he was not a good conversationalist, because he felt that he was not learned
enough. Neither was he a good listener. Putting
it a little strongly, he was often not even polite. If
present with others, or participating in a conversation, he was rather abrupt, and in his anxiety to say
something apt or to illustrate the subject under
discussion, would burst in with a story. In our
office I have known him to consume the whole forenoon relating stories. If a man came to see him
for the purpose of finding out something which he
did not care to let him know and at the same time
did not want to refuse him, he was very adroit. In
such cases Lincoln would do most of the talking,
swinging around what he suspected was the vital
point, but never nearing it, interlarding his answers
with a seemingly endless supply of stories and jokes.
The interview being both interesting and pleasant,
the man would depart in good humor, believing
he had accomplished his mission. After he had
walked away a few squares and had cooled off, the

question would come up, "Well, what did I find out?" Blowing away the froth of Lincoln's humorous narratives he would find nothing substantial left.

"As he entered the trial," relates one of his colleagues at the bar,* "where most lawyers would object he would say he 'reckoned' it would be fair to let this in, or that; and sometimes, when his adversary could not quite prove what Lincoln knew to be the truth, he 'reckoned' it would be fair to admit the truth to be so-and-so. When he did object to the court, and when he heard his objections answered, he would often say, 'Well, I reckon I must be wrong.' Now, about the time he had practised this three-fourths through the case, if his adversary didn't understand him, he would wake up in a few minutes learning that he had feared the Greeks too late and find himself beaten. He was wise as a serpent in the trial of a cause, but I have had too many scares from his blows to certify that he was harmless as a dove. When the whole thing was unravelled, the adversary would begin to see that what he was so blandly giving away was simply what he couldn't get and keep. By giving away six points and carrying the seventh he carried his case, and the whole case hanging on the seventh, he traded away everything which would give him the least aid in carrying that. Any man who took Lincoln for a simple-minded man would very soon wake up with his back in a ditch."

---

* Leonard Swett.

Lincoln's restless ambition found its gratification only in the field of politics. He used the law merely as a stepping-stone to what he considered a more attractive condition in the political world. In the allurements held out by the latter he seemed to be happy. Nothing in Lincoln's life has provoked more discussion than the question of his ability as a lawyer. I feel warranted in saying that he was at the same time a very great and a very insignificant lawyer. Judge David Davis, in his eulogy on Lincoln at Indianapolis, delivered at the meeting of the bar there in May, 1865, said this: "In all the elements that constituted a lawyer he had few equals. He was great at *nisi prius* and before an appellate tribunal. He seized the strong points of a cause and presented them with clearness and great compactness. His mind was logical and direct, and he did not indulge in extraneous discussion. Generalities and platitudes had no charm for him. An unfailing vein of humor never deserted him, and he was able to claim the attention of court and jury when the cause was most uninteresting by the appropriateness of his anecdotes. His power of comparison was large, and he rarely failed in a legal discussion to use that mode of reasoning. The framework of his mental and moral being was honesty, and a wrong case was poorly defended by him. The ability which some eminent lawyers possess of explaining away the bad points of a cause by ingenious sophistry was denied him. In order to bring into full activity his great powers it was necessary that he should be convinced of the right and justice of the matter which he advocated. When so convinced, whether the cause was great or small he was usually successful."*

This statement of Judge Davis in general is correct, but in some particulars is faulty. It was intended as a eulogy on Lincoln, and as such would not admit of as many limitations and modifications as if spoken under other circumstances. In 1866 Judge Davis said in a statement made to me in his home at Bloomington, which I still have, "Mr. Lincoln had no managing faculty nor organizing power; hence a child could conform to the simple and technical rules, the means and the modes of getting at justice better than he. The law has its own rules, and a student could get at them or keep with them better than Lincoln. Sometimes he was forced to study these if he could not get the rubbish of a case removed. But all the way through his lack of method and organizing ability was clearly apparent." The idea that Mr. Lincoln was a great lawyer in the higher courts and a good *nisi prius* lawyer, and yet that a child or student could manage a case in court better than he, seems strangely inconsistent, but the facts of his life as a lawyer will reconcile this and other apparent contradictions.

I was not only associated with Mr. Lincoln in Springfield, but was frequently on the circuit with

---

* He never took advantage of a man's low character to prejudice the jury. Mr. Lincoln thought his duty to his client extended to what was honorable and high-minded, just and noble—nothing further. Hence the meanest man at the bar always paid great deference and respect to him.—David Davis, Sept. 10, 1866, MS.

him, but of course not so much as Judge Davis, who held the court, and whom Lincoln followed around on the circuit for at least six months out of the year. I easily realized that Lincoln was strikingly deficient in the technical rules of the law. Although he was constantly reminding young legal aspirants to study and "work, work," yet I doubt if he ever read a single elementary law book through in his life. In fact, I may truthfully say, I never knew him to read through a law book of any kind. Practically he knew nothing of the rules of evidence, of pleading, or practice, as laid down in the text-books, and seemed to care nothing about them. He had a keen sense of justice, and struggled for it, throwing aside forms, methods, and rules, until it appeared pure as a ray of light flashing through a fog-bank. He was not a general reader in any field of knowledge, but when he had occasion to learn or investigate any subject he was thorough and indefatigable in his search. He not only went to the root of a question, but dug up the root, and separated and analyzed every fibre of it. He was in every respect a case lawyer, never cramming himself on any question till he had a case in which the question was involved. He thought slowly and acted slowly; he must needs have time to analyze all the facts in a case and wind them into a connected story. I have seen him lose cases of the plainest justice, which the most inexperienced member of the bar would have gained without effort. Two things were essential to his success in managing a case. One was time;

the other a feeling of confidence in the justice of
the cause he represented. He used to say, "If I
can free this case from technicalities and get it properly swung to the jury, I'll win it." But if either of
these essentials were lacking, he was the weakest
man at the bar. He was greatest in my opinion as
a lawyer in the Supreme Court of Illinois. There
the cases were never hurried. The attorneys generally prepared their cases in the form of briefs, and
the movements of the court and counsel were so
slow that no one need be caught by surprise. I was
with Lincoln once and listened to an oral argument
by him in which he rehearsed an extended history
of the law. It was a carefully prepared and masterly discourse, but, as I thought, entirely useless.
After he was through and we were walking home I
asked him why he went so far back in the history of
the law. I presumed the court knew enough history. "That's where you're mistaken," was his
instant rejoinder. "I dared not trust the case on the
presumption that the court knows everything—in
fact I argued it on the presumption that the court
didn't know anything," a statement which, when
one reviews the decision of our appellate courts, is
not so extravagent as one would at first suppose.

I used to grow restless at Lincoln's slow movements and speeches in court. "Speak with more
vim," I would frequently say, "and arouse the jury
—talk faster and keep them awake". In answer to
such a suggestion he one day made use of this illustration: "Give me your little pen-knife, with its
short blade, and hand me that old jack-knife, lying

on the table." Opening the blade of the pen-knife he said: "You see, this blade at the point travels rapidly, but only through a small portion of space till it stops; while the long blade of the jack-knife moves no faster but through a much greater space than the small one. Just so with the long, labored movements of my mind. I may not emit ideas as rapidly as others, because I am compelled by nature to speak slowly, but when I do throw off a thought it seems to me, though it comes with some effort, it has force enough to cut its own way and travel a greater distance." This was said to me when we were alone in our office simply for illustration. It was not said boastingly.

As a specimen of Lincoln's method of reasoning I insert here the brief or notes of an argument used by him in a lawsuit as late as 1858. I copy from the original.

"Legislation and adjudication must follow and conform to the progress of society.

"The progress of society now begins to produce cases of the transfer for debts of the entire property of railroad corporations; and to enable transferees to use and enjoy the transferred property *legislation* and *adjudication* begin to be necessary.

"Shall this class of legislation just now beginning with us be *general* or *special*?

"Section Ten of our Constitution requires that it should be general, if possible. (Read the Section.)

"Special legislation always trenches upon the judicial department; and in so far violates Section Two of the Constitution. (Read it.)

"Just reasoning—policy—is in favor of general legislation—else the legislature will be *loaded* down with the investigation of smaller cases—a work which the courts *ought* to perform, and can perform much more perfectly. How can the Legislature rightly decide the facts between P. & B. and S. C. & Co.

"It is said that under a general law, whenever a R. R. Co. gets tired of its debts, it may transfer *fraudulently* to get rid of them. So they may—so may individuals; and which—the *Legislature* or the courts—is best suited to try the question of fraud in either case?

"It is said, if a purchaser have acquired legal rights, let him not be robbed of them, but if he needs *legislation* let him submit to just terms to obtain it.

"Let him, say we, have general law in advance (guarded in every possible way against fraud), so that, when he acquires a legal right, he will have no occasion to wait for additional legislation; and if he has practiced fraud let the courts so decide."

David Davis said this of Lincoln: "When in a lawsuit he believed his client was oppressed,—as in the Wright case,—he was hurtful in denunciation. When he attacked meanness, fraud, or vice, he was powerful, merciless in his castigation." The Wright case referred to was a suit brought by Lincoln and myself to compel a pension agent to refund a portion of a fee which he had withheld from the widow of a revolutionary soldier. The entire pension was $400.00, of which sum the agent had retained one-half. The pensioner, an old woman crippled and bent with age, came hobbling into the office and told her story. It stirred Lincoln up, and he walked over to the agent's office and made a demand for a return of the money, but without success. Then suit was brought. The day before the trial I hunted up for Lincoln, at his request, a history of the Revolutionary War, of which he read a good portion. He told me to remain during the trial until I had heard his address to the jury. "For," said he, "I am going to skin Wright, and get that money back." The only witness we introduced was the old lady, who through her tears told her story. In his speech to the jury, Lincoln recounted the causes leading to the outbreak of the Revolutionary struggle, and then drew a vivid picture of the hardships of Valley Forge, describing with minuteness the men, barefooted and with bleeding feet, creeping over the ice. As he reached that point in his speech wherein he narrated the hardened action of the defendant in fleecing the old woman of her pension his eyes flashed, and throwing aside his handkerchief, which he held in his right hand, he fairly launched into him. His speech for the next five or ten minutes justified the declaration of Davis, that he was "hurtful in denunciation and merciless in castigation." There was no rule of court to restrain him in his argument, and I never, either on the stump or on other occasions in court, saw him so wrought up. Before he closed, he drew an ideal picture of the plaintiff's husband, the deceased soldier, parting with his wife at the threshold of their home, and kissing their little babe in the cradle, as he started for the war. "Time rolls by," he said, in conclusion; "the heroes of '76 have passed away and are encamped on the other

shore. The soldier has gone to rest, and now, crip-
pled, blinded, and broken, his widow comes to you
and to me, gentlemen of the jury, to right her
wrongs. She was not always thus. She was once a
beautiful young woman. Her step was as elastic, her
face as fair, and her voice as sweet as any that rang
in the mountains of old Virginia. But now she is
poor and defenceless. Out here on the prairies of
Illinois, many hundreds of miles away from the
scenes of her childhood, she appeals to us, who
enjoy the privileges achieved for us by the patriots
of the Revolution, for our sympathetic aid and
manly protection. All I ask is, shall we befriend
her?" The speech made the desired impression on
the jury. Half of them were in tears, while the defendant sat in the court room, drawn up and writh-
ing under the fire of Lincoln's fierce invective.
The jury returned a verdict in our favor for every
cent we demanded. Lincoln was so much interested in the old lady that he became her surety for
costs, paid her way home, and her hotel bill while
she was in Springfield. When the judgment was
paid we remitted the proceeds to her and made no
charge for our services. Lincoln's notes for the
argument were unique: "No contract.—Not professional services.—Unreasonable charge.—Money retained by Def't not given by Pl'ff.—Revolutionary
War.—Describe Valley Forge privations.—Ice—
Soldier's bleeding feet.—Pl'ffs husband.—Soldier
leaving home for army.—*Skin Def't.*—Close."

It must not be inferred from this that Lincoln
was in the habit of slopping over. He never

hunted up acts of injustice, but if they came to him he was easily enlisted. In 1855 he was attending court at the town of Clinton, Illinois. Fifteen ladies from a neighboring village in the county had been indicted for trespass. Their offence consisted in sweeping down on one Tanner, the keeper of a saloon in the village, and knocking in the heads of his barrels. Lincoln was not employed in the case, but sat watching the trial as it proceeded. In defending the ladies their attorney seemed to evince a little want of tact, and this prompted one of the former to invite Mr. Lincoln to add a few words to the jury, if he thought he could aid their cause. He was too gallant to refuse and, their attorney having consented, he made use of the following argument: "In this case I would change the order of indictment and have it read The State *vs.* Mr. Whiskey, instead of The State *vs.* The Ladies; and touching these there are three laws: The Law of self-protection; the law of the land, or statute law; and the moral law, or law of God. First, the law of self-protection is a law of necessity, as evinced by our forefathers in casting the tea overboard and asserting their right to the pursuit of life, liberty, and happiness. In this case it is the only defense the ladies have, for Tanner neither feared God nor regarded man. Second, the law of the land, or statute law, and Tanner is recreant to both. Third, the moral law, or law of God, and this is probably a law for the violation of which the jury can fix no punishment." Linciln gave some of his own observations on the ruinous effects of whiskey in society, and demanded its early suppression. After he had concluded, the Court, without awaiting the return of the jury, dismissed the ladies, saying: "Ladies, go home. I will require no bond of you, and if any fine is ever wanted of you, we will let you know."

After Lincoln's death a fellow-lawyer paid this tribute to him:* "He was wonderfully kind, careful, and just. He had an immense stock of common-sense, and he had faith enough in it to trust it in every emergency. Mr. Lincoln's love of justice and fair-play was his predominating trait. I have often listened to him when I thought he would certainly state his case out of court. It was not in his nature to assume or attempt to bolster up a false position.† He would abandon his case first.

---

* Joseph Gillespie, MS., Letter, Oct. 8, 1886.

† "Early in 1858 at Danville, Ill., I met Lincoln, Swett, and others who had returned from court in an adjoining county, and were discussing the various features of a murder trial in which Lincoln had made a vigorous fight for the prosecution and Swett had defended. The plea of the defense was insanity. On inquiring the name of the defendant I was surprised to learn that it was my old friend Isaac Wyant, formerly of Indiana. I told them that I had been Wyant's counsel frequently and had defended him from almost every charge in the calendar of crimes; and that he was a weak brother and could be led into almost everything. At once Lincoln began to manifest great interest in Wyant's history, and had to be told all about him. The next day on the way to the court-house he told me he had been greatly troubled over what I related about Wyant; that his sleep had been disturbed by the fear that he had been too bitter and unrelenting in his prosecution of him. "I acted," he said, "on the theory that he was 'possuming' insanity, and now I fear I have been too severe and that the poor fellow may be insane after all. If he cannot realize the wrong of his crime, then I was wrong in aiding to punish him.'" —Hon. Joseph E. McDonald, August, 1888. Statement to J. W. W.

He did so in the case of Buckmaster for the use of Dedham *vs.* Beems and Arthur, in our Supreme Court, in which I happened to be opposed to him. Another gentlemen, less fastidious, took Mr. Lincoln's place and gained the case."

A widow who owned a piece of valuable land employed Lincoln and myself to examine the title to the property, with the view of ascertaining whether certain alleged tax liens were just or not. In tracing back the title we were not satisfied with the description of the ground in one of the deeds of conveyance. Lincoln, to settle the matter, took his surveying instruments and surveyed the ground himself. The result proved that Charles Matheney, a former grantor, had sold the land at so much per acre, but that in describing it he had made an error and conveyed more land than he received pay for. This land descended to our client, and Lincoln after a careful survey and calculation, decided that she ought to pay to Matheney's heirs the sum which he had shown was due them by reason of the erroneous conveyance. To this she entered strenuous objections, but when assured that unless she consented to this act of plain justice we would drop the case, she finally, though with great reluctance, consented. She paid the required amount, and this we divided up into smaller sums proportioned to the number of heirs. Lincoln himself distributed these to the heirs, obtaining a receipt from each one.*

---

* "DEAR HERNDON:
"One morning, not long before Lincoln's nomination—a year perhaps—I was in your office and heard the following: Mr

While Mr. Lincoln was no financier and had no propensity to acquire property,—no avarice of the get,—yet he had the capacity of retention, or the avarice of the keep. He never speculated in lands or anything else. In the days of land offices and "choice lots in a growing town" he had many opportunities to make safe ventures promising good returns, but he never availed himself of them. His brother lawyers were making good investments and lucky turns, some of them, Davis, for example, were rapidly becoming wealthy; but Lincoln cared nothing for speculation; in fact there was no ventursome spirit in him. His habits were very simple. He was not fastidious as to food or dress. His hat was brown, faded, and the nap usually worn or rubbed off. He wore a short cloak and sometimes a shawl. His coat and vest hung loosely on his gaunt frame, and his trousers were invariably too short. On the

---

Lincoln, seated at the baize-covered table in the center of the office, listened attentively to a man who talked earnestly and in a low tone. After being thus engaged for some time Lincoln at length broke in, and I shall never forget his reply. 'Yes,' he said, 'we can doubtless gain your case for you; we can set a whole neighborhood at loggerheads; we can distress a widowed mother and her six fatherless children and thereby get for you six hundred dollars to which you seem to have a legal claim, but which rightfully belongs, it appears to me, as much to the woman and her children as it does to you. You must remember that some things legally right are not morally right. We shall not take your case, but will give you a little advice for which we will charge you nothing. You seem to be a sprightly, energetic man; we would advise you to try your hand at making six hundred dollars in some other way.'

"Yours,

"LORD."

From undated MS., about 1866.

circuit he carried in one hand a faded green umbrella, with "A. Lincoln" in large white cotton or muslin letters sewed on the inside. The knob was gone from the handle, and when closed a piece of cord was usually tied around it in the middle to keep it from flying open. In the other hand he carried a literal carpet-bag, in which were stored the few papers to be used in court, and underclothing enough to last till his return to Springfield. He slept in a long, coarse, yellow flannel shirt, which reached half-way between his knees and ankles. It probably was not made to fit his bony figure as completely as Beau Brummel's shirt, and hence we can somewhat appreciate the sensation of a young lawyer who, on seeing him thus arrayed for the first time, observed afterwards that, "He was the ungodliest figure I ever saw."

"He never complained of the food, bed, or lodgings. If every other fellow grumbled at the bill-of-fare which greeted us at many of the dingy taverns," says David Davis, "Lincoln said nothing." He was once presiding as judge in the absence of Davis, and the case before him was an action brought by a merchant against the father of a minor son for a suit of clothes sold to the son without parental authority. The real question was whether the clothes were necessary, and suited to the condition of the son's life. The father was a weatlhy farmer; the bill for the clothing was twenty-eight dollars. I happened in court just as Lincoln was rendering his decision. He ruled against the plea of necessity. "I have rarely in my

life," said he, "worn a suit of clothes costing
twenty-eight dollars."

"Several of us lawyers," remarked one of his colleagues, "in the eastern end of the circuit annoyed
Lincoln once while he was holding court for Davis
by attempting to defend against a note to which
there were many makers. We had no legal, but a
good moral defense, but what we wanted most of all
was to stave it off till the next term of court by one
expedient or another. We bothered "the court"
about it till late on Saturday, the day of adjournment. He adjourned for supper with nothing left
but this case to dispose of. After supper he heard
our twaddle for nearly an hour, and then made this
odd entry: 'L. D. Chaddon *vs.* J. D. Beasley *et al.*
April Term, 1856. Champaign County Court. Plea
in abatement by B. Z. Green, a defendant not
served, filed Saturday at 11 o'clock A. M., April 24,
1856, stricken from the files by order of court. De-
murrer to declaration, if there ever was one, over-
ruled. Defendants who are served now, at 8 o'clock,
P. M., of the last day of the term, ask to plead to
the merits, which is denied by the court on the
ground that the offer comes too late, and therefore, as by *nil dicet,* judgment is rendered for Pl'ff.
Clerk assess damages. A. Lincoln, Judge *pro
tem.*'" The lawyer who reads this singular entry
will appreciate its oddity if no one else does. After
making it one of the lawyers, on recovering his
astonishment, ventured to enquire, "Well, Lincoln,

---

* H. C. Whitney, MS., letter, Nov. 13, 1865.

how can we get this case up again?" Lincoln eyed him quizzically a moment, and then answered, "You have all been· so 'mighty smart about this case you can find out how to take it up again yourselves."*

The same gentleman who furnishes this last incident, and who was afterward a trusted friend of Mr. Lincoln, Henry C. Whitney, has described most happily the delights of a life on the circuit. A bit of it, referring to Lincoln, I apprehend, cannot be deemed out of place here. "In October, 1854, Abraham Lincoln," he relates, "drove into our town (Urbana) to attend court. He had the appearance of a rough, intelligent farmer, and his rude, home-made buggy and raw-boned horse enforced this belief. I had met him for the first time in June of the same year. David Davis and Leonard Swett had just preceded him. The next morning he

---

* "During my first attendance at court in Menard County," relates a lawyer who travelled the circuit with Lincoln, "some thirty young men had been indicted for playing cards, and Lincoln and I were employed in their defense. The prosecuting attorney, in framing the indictments, alternately charged the defendants with playing a certain game of cards called 'seven-up,' and in the next bill charged them with playing cards at a certain game called 'old sledge.' Four defendants were indicted in each bill. The prosecutor, being entirely unacquainted with games at cards, did not know the fact that both 'seven-up' and 'old sledge' were one and the same. Upon the trial on the bills describing the game as 'seven-up' our witnesses would swear that the game played was 'old sledge,' and vice versa on the bills alleging the latter. The result was an acquittal in every case under the instructions of the Court. The prosecutor never found out the dodge until the trials were over, and immense fun and rejoicing were indulged in at the result."

started North, on the Illinois Central Railroad, and
as he went in an old omnibus he played on a boy's
harp all the way to the depot. I used to attend
the Danville court, and while there, usually roomed
with Lincoln and Davis. We stopped at McCormick's hotel, an old-fashioned frame country tavern.
Jurors, counsel, prisoners, everybody ate at a long
table. The judge, Lincoln, and I had the ladies'
parlor fitted up with two beds. Lincoln, Swett,
McWilliams, of Bloomington, Voorhees, of Coving-
ton, Ind., O. L. Davis, Drake, Ward Lamon, Lawrence, Beckwith, and O. F. Harmon, of Danville,
Whiteman, of Iroquois County, and Chandler, of
Williamsport, Ind., constituted the bar. Lincoln,
Davis, Swett, I, and others who came from the
western part of the state would drive from Urbana.
The distance was thirty-six miles. We sang and
exchanged stories all the way. We had no hesitation in stopping at a farm-house and ordering
them to kill and cook a chicken for dinner. By
dark we reached Danville. Lamon would have
whiskey in his office for the drinking ones, and those
who indulged in petty gambling would get by
themselves and play till late in the night. Lincoln,
Davis, and a few local wits would spend the evening
in Davis's room, talking politics, wisdom, and fun.
Lincoln and Swett were the great lawyers, and
Lincoln always wanted Swett in jury cases.
We who stopped at the hotel would all breakfast
together and frequently go out into the woods and
hold court. We were of more consequence than
a court and bar is now. The feelings were those of

great fraternity in the bar, and if we desired to re-
strict our circle it was no trouble for Davis to freeze
out any disagreeable persons. Lincoln was fond of
going all by himself to any little show or concert.
I have known him to slip away and spend the entire
evening at a little magic lantern show intended for
children. A travelling concert company, calling
themselves the 'Newhall Family,' were sure of
drawing Lincoln. One of their number, Mrs. Hil-
lis, a good singer, he used to tell us was the only
woman who ever seemed to exhibit any liking for
him. I attended a negro-minstrel show in Chicago,
where we heard Dixie sung. It was entirely new,
and pleased him greatly. In court he was irrepressible and apparently inexhaustible in his fund of
stories. Where in the world a man who had
travelled so little and struggled amid the restric-
tions of such limited surroundings could gather up
such apt and unique yarns we never could guess.
Davis appreciated Lincoln's talent in this direction,
and was always ready to stop business to hear one
of his stories. Lincoln was very bashful when in
the presence of ladies. I remember once we were
invited to take tea at a friend's house, and while in
the parlor I was called to the front gate to see a
client. When I returned, Lincoln, who had under-
taken to entertain the ladies, was twisting and
squirming in his chair, and as bashful as a school-
boy. Everywhere, though we met a hard crowd at
every court, and though things were free and easy,
we were treated with great respect."

Probably the most important lawsuit Lincoln

and I conducted was one in which we defended the
Illinois Central Railroad in an action brought by
McLean County, Illinois, in August, 1853, to recover
taxes alleged to be due the county from the road.
The Legislature had granted the road immunity
from taxation, and this was a case intended
to test the constitutionality of the law. The
road sent a retainer fee of $250. In the lower court
the case was decided in favor of the railroad. An
appeal to the Supreme Court followed, and there it
was argued twice, and finally decided in our favor.
This last decision was rendered some time in 1855.
Mr. Lincoln soon went to Chicago and presented
our bill for legal services. We only asked for
$2,000 more. The official to whom he was referred,
—supposed to have been the superintendent George
B. McClellan who afterwards became the eminent
general,—looking at the bill expressed great surprise. "Why, sir," he exclaimed, "this is as much
as Daniel Webster himself would have charged.
We cannot allow such a claim." Stung by the re-
buff, Lincoln withdrew the bill, and started for
home. On the way he stopped at Bloomington.
There he met Grant Goodrich, Archibald Williams,
Norman B. Judd, O. H. Browning, and other
attorneys, who, on learning of his modest charge
for such valuable services rendered the railroad,
induced him to increase the demand to $5,000,
and to bring suit for that sum. This was done at
once. On the trial six lawyers certified that the
bill was reasonable, and judgment for that sum
went by default. The judgment was promptly paid.

Lincoln gave me my half, and much as we deprecated the avarice of great corporations, we both thanked the Lord for letting the Illinois Central Railroad fall into our hands.

In the summer of 1857 Lincoln was employed by one Manny, of Chicago, to defend him in an action brought by McCormick,*who was the inventor of the reaping machine, for infringement of patent. Lincoln had been recommended to Manny by E. B. Washburne, then a member of Congress from northern Illinois. The case was to be tried before Judge McLean at Cincinnati, in the Circuit Court of the United States. The counsel for McCormick was Reverdy Johnson. Edwin M. Stanton and George Harding, of Philadelphia, were associated on the other side with Lincoln. The latter came to Cincinnati a few days before the argument took place, and stopped at the house of a friend. "The case was one of great importance pecuniarily," relates a lawyer† in Cincinnati, who was a member of the bar at the time, "and in the law questions involved. Reverdy Johnson represented the plaintiff. Mr. Lincoln had prepared himself with the greatest care; his ambition was up to speak in the case and to measure swords with the renowned lawyer from Baltimore. It was understood between his client and himself before his coming that Mr. Harding, of Philadelphia, was to be associated with him in the case, and was to make the 'mechanical argument.'

---

* The case, McCormick *vs.* Manny, is reported in 6 McLean's Rep., p. 539.
† W. M. Dickson.

After reaching Cincinnati, Mr. Lincoln was a little surprised and annoyed to learn that his client had also associated with him Mr. Edwin M. Stanton, of Pittsburg, and a lawyer of our own bar, the reason assigned being that the importance of the case required a man of the experience and power of Mr. Stanton to meet Mr. Johnson. The Cincinnati lawyer was appointed for his 'local influence.' These reasons did not remove the slight conveyed in the employment without consultation with him of this additional counsel. He keenly felt it, but acquiesced. The trial of the case came on; the counsel for defense met each morning for consultation. On one of these occasions one of the counsel moved that only two of them should speak in the case. This matter was also acquiesced in. It had always been understood that Mr. Harding was to speak to explain the mechanism of the reapers. So this motion excluded either Mr. Lincoln or Mr. Stanton, —which? By the custom of the bar, as between counsel of equal standing, and in the absence of any action of the client, the original counsel speaks. By this rule Mr. Lincoln had precedence. Mr. Stanton suggested to Mr. Lincoln to make the speech. Mr. Lincoln answered. 'No, you speak.' Mr. Stanton replied, 'I will,' and taking up his hat, said he would go and make preparation. Mr. Lincoln acquiesced in this, but was greatly grieved and mortified; he took but little more interest in the case, though remaining until the conclusion of the trial. He seemed to be greatly depressed, and gave evidence of that tendency to melancholy which so marked his character. His parting on leaving the city cannot be forgotten. Cordially shaking the hand of his hostess he said: 'You have made my stay here most agreeable, and I am a thousand times obliged to you; but in reply to your request for me to come again, I must say to you I never expect to be in Cincinnati again. I have nothing against the city, but things have so happened here as to make it undesirable for me ever to return.' Lincoln felt that Stanton had not only been very discourteous to him, but had purposely ignored him in the case, and that he had received rather rude, if not unkind, treatment from all hands. Stanton, in his brusque and abrupt way, it is said, described him as a 'long, lank creature from Illinois, wearing a dirty linen duster for a coat, on the back of which the perspiration had splotched wide stains that resembled a map of the continent. Mr. Lincoln," adds Mr. Dickson, "remained in Cincinnati about a week, moving freely around, yet not twenty men knew him personally or knew he was here; not a hundred would have known who he was had his name been given to them. He came with the fond hope of making fame in a forensic contest with Reverdy Johnson. He was pushed aside, humilated and mortified. He attached to the innocent city the displeasure that filled his bosom, and shook its dust from his feet." On his return to Springfield he was somewhat reticent regarding the trial, and, contrary to his custom, communicated to his associates at the bar but few of its incidents. He told me that he had been

"roughly handled by that man Stanton"; that
he overheard the latter from an adjoining room,
while the door was slightly ajar, referring to Lincoln, inquire of another, "Where did that long-
armed creature come from, and what can he expect
to do in this case?" During the trial Lincoln
formed a poor opinion of Judge McLean. He
characterized him as an "old granny," with considerable vigor of mind, but no perception at all. "If
you were to point your finger at him," he put it,
"and a darning needle at the same time he never
would know which was the sharpest."

As Lincoln grew into public favor and achieved
such marked success in the profession, half the bar
of Springfield began to be envious of his growing
popularity. I believe there is less jealousy and bitter feeling among lawyers than professional men of
any other class; but it should be borne in mind that
in that early day a portion of the bar in every
county seat, if not a majority of the lawyers everywhere, were politicians. Stuart frequently differed
from Lincoln on political questions, and was full
of envy. Likewise those who coincided with
Lincoln in his political views were disturbed in the
same way. Even Logan was not wholly free from
the degrading passion. But in this respect Lincoln
suffered no more than other great characters who
preceded him in the world's history.

That which Lincoln's adversaries in a lawsuit
feared most of all was his apparent disregard of
custom or professional propriety in managing a
case before a jury. He brushed aside all rules, and

very often resorted to some strange and strategic
performance which invariably broke his opponent
down or exercised some peculiar influence over the
jury. Hence the other side in a case were in constant fear of one of his dramatic strokes, or trem-
bled lest he should "ring in" some ingeniously
planned interruption not on the programme. In a
case where Judge Logan—always earnest and grave
—opposed him, Lincoln created no little merriment
by his reference to Logan's style of dress. He
carried the surprise in store for the latter, till
he reached his turn before the jury. Addressing
them, he said: "Gentlemen, you must be careful
and not permit yourselves to be overcome by the
eloquence of counsel for the defense. Judge Logan,
I know, is an effective lawyer. I have met him
too often to doubt that; but shrewd and careful
though he be, still he is sometimes wrong. Since
this trial has begun I have discovered that, with
all his caution and fastidiousness, he hasn't knowledge enough to put his shirt on right." Logan
turned red as crimson, but sure enough, Lincoln
was correct, for the former had donned a new shirt,
and by mistake had drawn it over his head with the
pleated bosom behind. The general laugh which
followed destroyed the effect of Logan's eloquence
over the jury—the very point at which Lincoln
aimed.

The trial of William Armstrong* for the murder

---

* This incident in Lincoln's career has been most happily uti-
lized by Dr. Edward Eggleston in his story "The Graysons,"
recently published in the *Century Magazine.*

of James P. Metzger, in May, 1858, at Beardstown, Illinois, in which Lincoln secured the acquittal of the defendant, was one of the gratifying triumphs in his career as a lawyer. Lincoln's defense, wherein he floored the principal prosecuting witness, who had testified positively to seeing the fatal blow struck in the moonlight, by showing from an almanac that the moon had set, was not more convincing than his eloquent and irresistible appeal in his client's favor. The latter's mother, old Hannah Armstrong, the friend of his youth, had solicited him to defend her son. "He told the jury," relates the prosecuting attorney, "of his once being a poor, friendless boy; that Armstrong's parents took him into their house, fed and clothed him, and gave him a home. There were tears in his eyes as he spoke. The sight of his tall, quivering frame, and the particulars of the story he so pathetically told, moved the jury to tears also, and they forgot the guilt of the defendant in their admiration of his advocate. It was the most touching scene I ever witnessed."[*] Before passing it may be well to listen to the humble tribute of old Hannah Armstrong, the defendant's mother: "Lincoln had said to me, 'Hannah, your son will be cleared before sundown.' I left the court-room, and they came and told me that my son was cleared and a free man. I went up to the court-house. The jury shook hands with me; so did the judge and Lincoln; tears streamed down Lincoln's eyes . . . . After the trial I asked him

---

* J. Henry Shaw, letter, Aug. 22, 1866, MS.

what his fee would be; told him I was poor. 'Why, Hannah,' he said, 'I sha'n't charge you a cent, and anything else I can do for you, will do it willingly and without charge.' He afterwards wrote to me about a piece of land which certain men were trying to get from me, and said: 'Hannah, they can't get your land. Let them try it in the Circuit Court, and then you appeal it; bring it to the Supreme Court and I and Herndon will attend to it for nothing.' "*

The last suit of any importance in which Lincoln was personally engaged, was known as the Johnson sand-bar case. It involved the title to certain lands, the accretion on the shores of Lake Michigan, in or near Chicago. It was tried in the United States Circuit Court at Chicago in April and May, 1860. During the trial, the Court—Judge Drummond—and all the counsel on both sides dined at the residence of Isaac N. Arnold, afterwards a member of Congress. "Douglas and Lincoln," relates Mr. Arnold, "were at the time both candidates for the nomination for President. There were active and ardent political friends of each at the table, and when the sentiment was proposed, 'May Illinois furnish the next President,' it was drank with enthusiasm by the friends of both Lincoln and Douglas."†

I could fill this volume with reminiscences of Lincoln's career as a lawyer, but lest the reader should tire of what must savor in many cases of monotony

* From statement, Nov. 24, 1865.
† Arnold's "Lincoln," p. 90.

it is best to move on. I have made this portion of the book rather full; but as Lincoln's individuality and peculiarities were more marked in the law office and court-room than anywhere else it will play its part in making up the picture of the man. Enough has been told to show how, in the face of adverse fortune and the lack of early training and by force of his indomitable will and self-confidence, he gained such ascendency among the lawyers of Illinois. The reader is enabled thereby to understand the philosophy of his growth.

But now another field is preparing to claim him. There will soon be great need for his clear reason, masterly mind and heroic devotion to principle. The distant mutterings of an approaching contest are driving scattered factions into a union of sentiment and action. As the phalanxes of warriors are preparing for action, amid the rattle of forensic musketry, Lincoln, their courageous leader, equipped for battle, springs into view.

CHAPTER XII.

While Lincoln in a certain sense was buried in the law from the time his career in Congress closed till, to use his own words, "the repeal of the Missouri Compromise aroused him again," yet he was a careful student of his times and kept abreast of the many and varied movements in politics. He was generally on the Whig electoral tickets, and made himself heard during each successive canvas,*

---

* In the campaign of 1852, when Pierce was the Democratic candidate for President, Douglas made speeches for him in almost every State in the Union. His "key-note" was sounded at Richmond, Va. Lincoln, whose reputation was limited by the boundaries of Illinois, was invited by the Scott Club of Springfield to answer it, but his soul and heart were not in the undertaking. He had not yet been awakened, and, considering it entire, the speech was a poor effort. Another has truthfully said of it, "If it was distinguished by one quality above another it was by its attempts at humor, and all those attempts were strained and affected, as well as very coarse. He displayed a jealous and petulant temper from the first to the last, wholly beneath the dignity of the occasion and the importance of the topic. Considered as a whole it may be said that none of his public performances was more unworthy of its really noble author than this one. The closing paragraph will serve as a fair sample of the entire speech: "Let us stand by our candidate [Gen. Scott] as faithfully as he has always stood by our country, and I much doubt if we do not perceive a slight abatement of Judge Douglas's confidence in Providence as well as the people. I suspect that confidence is not more firmly fixed with the Judge than it was with the old woman whose horse

but he seemed to have lost that zealous interest in politics which characterized his earlier days. He plodded on unaware of, and seemingly without ambition. for, the great distinction that lay in store for him. John T. Stuart relates* that, as he and Lincoln were returning from the court in Tazewell county in 1850, and were nearing the little town of Dillon, they engaged in a discussion of the political situation. "As we were coming down the hill," are Stuart's words, "I said, 'Lincoln, the time is coming when we shall have to be all either Abolitionists or Democrats.' He thought a moment and then answered, ruefully and emphatically, 'When that time comes my mind is made up, for I believe the slavery question can never be successfully compromised.' I responded with equal emphasis, 'My mind is made up too.' " Thus it was with Lincoln. But he was too slow to suit the impetuous demand of the few pronounced Abolitionists whom he met in his daily walks. The sentiment of the majority in Springfield tended in the other direction, and thus environed, Lincoln lay down like the sleeping lion. The future would yet arouse him. At that time I was an ardent Abolitionist in sentiment. I used to warn Lincoln against his apparent conservatism when the needs of the hour were so great; but his only answer would be, 'Billy, you're

---

ran away with her in a buggy. She said she trusted in Providence till the 'britchen' broke, and then she didn't know what on 'airth' to do. The chance is the Judge will see the 'britchen' broke, and then he can at his leisure bewail the fate of Locofocoism as the victim of misplaced confidence."

   * Statement, J. T. S., MS., July 21, 1865.

too rampant and spontaneous.' I was in correspondence with Sumner, Greely, Phillips, and Garrison, and was thus thoroughly imbued with all the
rancor drawn from such strong anti-slavery sources.
I adhered to Lincoln, relying on the final outcome of
his sense of justice and right. Every time a good
speech on the great issue was made I sent for it.
Hence you could find on my table the latest utterances of Giddings, Phillips, Sumner, Seward, and
one whom I considered grander than all the others
—Theodore Parker. Lincoln and I took such
papers as the Chicago *Tribune*, New York *Tribune*,
Anti-Slavery Standard, *Emancipator*, and *National
Era*. On the other side of the question we took the
Charleston *Mercury* and the Richmond *Enquirer*.
I also bought a book called "Sociology," written
by one Fitzhugh, which defended and justified
slavery in every conceivable way. In addition I pur-
chased all the leading histories of the slavery movement, and other works which treated on that subject.
Lincoln himself never bought many books, but he
and I both read those I have named. After reading them we would discuss the questions they
touched upon and the ideas they suggested, from
our different points of view. I was never conscious
of having made much of an impression on Mr. Lincoln, nor do I believe I ever changed his views.
I will go further and say, that, from the profound
nature of his conclusions and the labored method
by which he arrived at them, no man is entitled to
the credit of having changed or greatly modi-
fied them. I remember once, after having read one

of Theodore Parker's sermons on slavery, saying to Mr. Lincoln substantially this: "I have always noticed that ill-gotten wealth does no man any good. This is as true of nations as individuals. I believe that all the ill-gotten gain wrenched by us from the negro through his enslavement will eventually be taken from us, and we will be set back where we began." Lincoln thought my prophecy rather direful. He doubted seriously if either of us would live to see the righting of so great a wrong; but years after, when writing his second Inaugural address, he endorsed the idea. Clothing it in the most beautiful language, he says: "Yet if God wills that it [the war] continue till all the wealth piled by the bondsman's two hundred and fifty years of unrequited toil shall be sunk, and until every drop of blood drawn by the lash shall be paid by another drawn by the sword, as was said three thousand years ago, so still it must be said, 'The judgments of the Lord are true and righteous altogether.' "

The passage in May, 1854, of the Kansas-Nebraska bill swept out of sight the Missouri Compromise and the Compromise measures of 1850. This bill, designed and carried through by Douglas, was regarded by him as the masterpiece of all his varied achievements in legislation. It served to prove more clearly than anything he had ever before done his flexibility and want of political conscience. Although in years gone before he had invoked the vengeance of Heaven on the ruthless hand that should dare to disturb the sanctity of the compact of 1821, yet now he was the arrogant and audacious

leader in the very work he had so heartily condemned. When we consider the bill and the unfortunate results which followed it in the border States
we are irresistibly led to conclude that it was, all
things considered, a great public wrong and a most
lamentable piece of political jugglery. The stump
speech which Thomas H. Benton charged that
Douglas had "injected into the belly of the bill"
contains all there was of Popular Sovereignty—"It
being the true intent and meaning of this act not
to legislate slavery into any Territory or State nor
to exclude it therefrom, but to leave the people
thereof perfectly free to form and regulate their
domestic institutions in their own way, subject only
to the Constitution of the United States," an
argument which, using Lincoln's words, "amounts
to this: That if any one man chooses to enslave
another no third man shall be allowed to object."
The widespread feeling the passage of this law
aroused everywhere over the Union is a matter of
general history. It stirred up in New England
the latent hostility to the aggression of slavery; it
stimulated to extraordinary endeavors the derided
Abolitionists, arming them with new weapons; it
sounded the death-knell of the gallant old Whig
party; it drove together strange, discordant elements
it readiness to fight a common enemy; it brought
to the forefront a leader in the person of Lincoln.

The revolt of Cook, Judd, and Palmer, all young
and progressive, from the Democratic majority in
the Legislature was the first sign of discontent in
Illinois. The rude and partly hostile reception of

Douglas, on his arrival in Chicago, did not in any degree tend to allay the feeling of disapproval so general in its manifestation. The warriors, young and old, removed their armor from the walls, and began preparations for the impending conflict. Lincoln had made a few speeches in aid of Scott during the campaign of 1852, but they were efforts entirely unworthy of the man. Now, however, a live issue was presented to him. No one realized this sooner than he. In the office discussions he grew bolder in his utterances. He insisted that the social and political difference between slavery and freedom was becoming more marked; that one must overcome the other; and that postponing the struggle between them would only make it the more deadly in the end. "The day of compromise," he still contended, "has passed. These two great ideas have been kept apart only by the most artful means. They are like two wild beasts in sight of each other, but chained and held apart. Some day these deadly antagonists will one or the other break their bonds, and then the question will be settled." In a conversation with a fellow-lawyer* he said of slavery: "It is the most glittering, ostentatious, and displaying property in the world, and now, if a young man goes courting, the only inquiry is how many negroes he or his lady-love owns. The love for slave property is swallowing up every other mercenary possession. Slavery is a great and crying injustice—an enormous national crime." At another time he made the

---

* Joseph Gillespie, MS. letter, June 9, '66.

observation that it was "singular that the courts
would hold that a man never lost his right to his
property that had been stolen from him, but that
he instantly lost his right to himself if he was
stolen." It is useless to add more evidence—for
it could be piled mountain high—showing that at
the very outset Mr. Lincoln was sound to the core
on the injustice and crime of human slavery.

After a brief rest at his home in Chicago Mr.
Douglas betook himself to the country, and in October, during the week of the State Fair, we find
him in Springfield. On Tuesday he made a speech
in the State House which, in view of the hostile
attitude of some of his own party friends, was a
labored defense of his position. It was full of ingenious sophistry and skilful argument. An unprec-
edented concourse of people had gathered from all
parts of the State, and Douglas, fresh from the halls
of Congress, was the lion of the hour. On the following day Mr. Lincoln, as the champion of the
opponents of Popular Sovereignty, was selected to
represent those who disagreed with the new legislation, and to answer Douglas. His speech encouraged
his friends no less than it startled his enemies. At
this time I was zealously interested in the new
movement, and not less so in Lincoln. I frequently
wrote the editorials in the Springfield *Journal,* the
editor, Simeon Francis, giving to Lincoln and to me
the utmost liberty in that direction. Occasionally
Lincoln would write out matter for publication, but
I believe I availed myself of the privilege oftener
than he. The editorial in the issue containing the

speeches of Lincoln and Douglas on this occasion
was my own, and while in description it may seem
rather strongly imbued with youthful enthusiasm,
yet on reading it in maturer years I am still inclined
to believe it reasonably faithful to the facts and
the situation. "The anti-Nebraska speech of Mr.
Lincoln," says the article, "was the profoundest in
our opinion that he has made in his whole life. He
felt upon his soul the truths burn which he uttered,
and all present felt that he was true to his own soul.
His feelings once or twice swelled within, and came
near stifling utterance. He quivered with emotion.
The whole house was as still as death. He attacked
the Nebraska bill with unusual warmth and energy;
and all felt that a man of strength was its enemy,
and that he intended to blast it if he could by
strong and manly efforts. He was most successful,
and the house approved the glorious triumph of
truth by loud and continued huzzas. Women
waved their white handkerchiefs in token of woman's silent but heartfelt assent. Douglas felt
the sting; the animal within him was roused because he frequently interrupted Mr. Lincoln. His
friends felt that he was crushed by Lincoln's powerful argument, manly logic, and illustrations from
nature around us. The Nebraska bill was shivered,
and like a tree of the forest was torn and rent asun-
der by the hot bolts of truth. Mr. Lincoln exhibited Douglas in all the attitudes he could be placed,
in a friendly debate. He exhibited the bill in all its
aspects to show its humbuggery and falsehood, and,
when thus torn to rags, cut into slips, held up

to the gaze of the vast crowd, a kind of scorn and mockery was visible upon the face of the crowd and upon the lips of their most eloquent speaker. At the conclusion of this speech every man and child felt that it was unanswerable. He took the heart captive and broke like a sun over the understanding."

Anent the subject of editorial writing it may not be inappropriate to relate that Lincoln and I both kept on furnishing political matter of many varieties for the Springfield *Journal* until 1860. Many of the editorials that I wrote were intended directly or indirectly to promote the interest of Lincoln. I wrote one on the advisability of annexing Cuba to the United States, taking the rather advanced ground that slavery would be abolished in Cuba before it would in this country—a position which aroused no little controversy with other papers. One little incident occurs to me in this connection which may not be without interest to newspaper men. A newspaper had been started in Springfield called the *Conservative*, which, it was believed, was being run in the interest of the Democratic party. While pretending to support Fillmore it was kept alive by Buchanan men and other kindred spirits, who were somewhat pro-slavery in their views. The thing was damaging Lincoln and the friends of freedom more than an avowed Democratic paper could. The editor, an easy, good-natured fellow, simply placed in charge to execute the will of those who gave the paper its financial backing, was a good friend of mine, and by means of this friendship I was always well informed of matters in the *Conservative* editorial room. One day I read in the Richmond *Enquirer* an article endorsing slavery, and arguing that from principle the enslavement of either whites or blacks was justifiable and right. I showed it to Lincoln, who remarked that it was "rather rank doctrine for Northern Democrats to endorse. I should like to see," he said, with emphasis, "some of these Illinois newspapers champion that." I told him if he would only wait and keep his own counsel I would have a pro-slavery organ in Springfield publish that very article. He doubted it, but when I told him how it was to be done he laughed and said, "Go in." I cut the slip out and succeeded in getting it in the paper named. Of course it was a trick, but it acted admirably. Its appearance in the new organ, although without comment, almost ruined that valuable journal, and my good-natured friend the editor was nearly overcome by the denunciation of those who were responsible for the organ's existence. My connection, and Lincoln's too,—for he endorsed the trick,—with the publication of the condemned article was eventually discovered, and we were thereafter effectually prevented from getting another line in the paper. The anti-slavery people quoted the article as having been endorsed by a Demoratic newspaper in Springfield, and Linoln himself used it with telling effect. He joined in the popular denunciation, expressing great astonishment that such a sentiment could find lodgment in any paper in Illinois,

although he knew full well how the whole thing
had been carried through.

During the remainder of the State-Fair week,
speeches were .made by Lyman Trumbull, Sidney
Breese, E. D. Taylor, and John Calhoun, none of
which unfortunately have been preserved. Among
those who mingled in the crowd and listened to
them was Owen Lovejoy, a radical, fiery, brave,
fanatical man, it may be, but one full of the virus of
Abolitionism. I had been thoroughly inoculated
with the latter myself, and so had many others, who
helped to swell the throng. The Nebraska movement had kindled anew the old zeal, and inspired us
with renewed confidence to begin the crusade. As
many of us as could, assembled together to organ-
ize for the campaign before us. As soon therefore
as Lincoln finished his speech in the hall of the
House of Representatives, Lovejoy, moving forward
from the crowd, announced a meeting in the same
place that evening of all the friends of Freedom.
That of course meant the Abolitionists with whom
I had been in conference all the day. Their plan
had been to induce Mr. Lincoln to speak for them
at their meeting. Strong as I was in the faith, yet
I doubted the propriety of Lincoln's taking any
stand yet. As I viewed it, he was ambitious to
climb to the United States Senate, and on grounds
of policy it would not do for him to occupy at that
time such advanced ground as we were taking. On
the other hand, it was equally as dangerous to
refuse a speech for the Abolitionists. I did not
know how he felt on the subject, but on learning

that Lovejoy intended to approach him with an
invitation, I hunted up Lincoln and urged him to
avoid meeting the enthusiastic champion of Abolitionism. "Go home at once," I said. "Take Bob
with you and drive somewhere into the country and
stay till this thing is over." Whether my admonition and reasoning moved him or not I do not
know, but it only remains to state that under pretence of having business in Tazewell county he
drove out of town in his buggy, and did not return
till the apostles of Abolitionism had separated and
gone to their homes.* I have always believed this
little arrangement—it would dignify it too much to
call it a plan—saved Lincoln. If he had endorsed
the resolutions passed at the meeting, or spoken simply in favor of freedom that night, he would have
been identified with all the rancor and extremes of
Abolitionism. If, on the contrary, he had been
invited to join them, and then had refused to take
a position as advanced as theirs, he would have lost
their support. In either event he was in great danger; and so he who was aspiring to succeed his old
rival, James Shields, in the United States Senate was
forced to avoid the issue by driving hastily in his one
horse buggy to the court in Tazewell county. A
singular coincidence suggests itself in the fact that,
twelve years before, James Shields and a friend
drove hastily in the same direction, and destined for
the same point, to force Lincoln to take issue in
another and entirely different matter.

---

* See Lincoln's Speech, Joint Debate, Ottawa, Ills., Aug. 20,
1858.

By request of party friends Lincoln was induced
to follow after Douglas and, at the various places
where the latter had appointments to speak, reply
to him. On the 16th of October they met at
Peoria, where Douglas enjoyed the advantages
of an "open and close." Lincoln made an effective speech, which he wrote out and furnished to
the Sangamon *Journal* for publication, and which can
be found among his public utterances. His party
friends in Springfield and elsewhere, who had urged
him to push after Douglas till he cried, "enough,"
were surprised a few days after the Peoria debate
to find him at home, with the information that by
an agreement with the latter they were both to
return home and speak no more during the campaign. Judge of his astonishment a few days later
to find that his rival, instead of going direct to his
home in Chicago, had stopped at Princeton and
violated his express agreement by making a speech
there! Lincoln was much displeased at this action of
Douglas, which tended to convince him that the latter was really a man devoid of fixed political morals. I remember his explanation in our office made
to me, William Butler, William Jayne, Ben. F.
Irwin, and other friends, to account for his early
withdrawal from the stump. After the Peoria debate
Douglas approached him and flattered him by saying that he was giving him more trouble on the
territorial and slavery questions than all the United
States Senate, and he therefore proposed to him
that both should abandon the field and return to
their homes. Now Lincoln could never refuse a

polite request—one in which no principle was
involved. I have heard him say, "It's a fortunate thing I wasn't born a woman, for I cannot
refuse anything, it seems." He therefore consented
to the cessation of debate proposed by Douglas, and
the next day both went to the town of Lacon, where
they had been billed for speeches. Their agreement was kept from their friends, and both declined
to speak—Douglas, on the ground of hoarseness,
and Lincoln gallantly refusing to take advantage of
"Judge Douglas's indisposition." Here they separated, Lincoln going directly home, and Douglas,
as before related, stopping at Princeton and collid-
ing in debate with Owen Lovejoy. Upon being
charged afterwards with his breech of agreement
Douglas responded that Lovejoy "bantered and
badgered" him so persistently he could not grace-
fully resist the encounter. The whole thing thoroughly displeased Lincoln.*

During this campaign Lincoln was nominated and
elected to the Legislature. This was done in the
face of his unwillingness and over his protest. On

---

* In a letter from Princeton, Ill., March 15, 1866, John H.
Bryant, brother of the poet William Cullen Bryant, writes: "I
have succeeded in finding an old file of our Princeton papers,
from which I learn that Mr. Douglas spoke here on Wednesday,
Oct. 18, 1854. This fixes the date. I recollect that he staid at
Tiskilwa, six miles south of this, the night before, and a number of our Democrats went down the next morning and escorted
him to this place. Douglas spoke first one half-hour and was
answered by Lovejoy one half-hour, when Douglas talked till
dark, giving no opportunity for reply.
                              "Yours truly,
                                   "JOHN H. BRYANT."

the ticket with him was Judge Logan. Both were elected by a majority of about 600 votes. Lincoln, being ambitious to reach the United States Senate, and warmly encouraged in his aspirations by his wife, resigned his seat in the Legislature in order that he might the more easily be elected to succeed his old rival James Shields, who was then one of the senators from Illinois. His canvass for that exalted office was marked by his characteristic activity and vigilance. During the anxious moments that intervened between the general election and the assembling of the Legislature he slept, like Napoleon, with one eye open. While attending court at Clinton on the 11th of November, a few days after the election, he wrote to a party friend in the town of Paris: "I have a suspicion that a Whig has been elected to the Legislature from Edgar. If this is not so, why then, '*nix cum arous;*' but if it is so, then could you not make a mark with him for me for U. S. Senator? I really have some chance. Please write me at Springfield giving me the names, post-offices, and political positions of your Representative and Senator, whoever they may be. Let this be confidential."*

That man who thinks Lincoln calmly sat down and gathered his robes about him, waiting for the people to call him, has a very erroneous knowledge of Lincoln. He was always calculating, and always planning ahead. His ambition was a little engine that knew no rest. The vicissitudes of a

---

* Robert Mosely, November 11, 1855, MS.

political campaign brought into play all his tact and management and developed to its fullest extent his latent industry. In common with other politicians he never overlooked a newspaper man who had it in his power to say a good or bad thing of him. The press of that day was not so powerful an institution as now, but ambitious politicians courted the favor of a newspaper man with as much zeal as the same class of men have done in later days. I remember a letter Lincoln once wrote to the editor of an obscure little country newspaper in southern Illinois in which he warms up to him in the following style.* "Friend Harding: I have been reading your paper for three or four years and have paid you nothing for it." He then encloses ten dollars and adminishes the editor with innocent complacency: "Put it into your pocket, saying nothing further about it." Very soon thereafter, he prepared an article on political matters and sent it to the rural journalist, requesting its publication in the editorial columns of his "valued paper," but the latter, having followed Lincoln's directions and stowed the ten dollars away in his pocket, and alive to the importance of his journal's influence, declined, "because," he said, "I long ago made it a rule to publish nothing as editorial matter not written by himself." Lincoln read the editor's answer to me. Although the laugh was on Lincoln he enjoyed the joke heartily. "That editor," he said, "has a rather lofty but proper conception of true journalism."

---

* Jacob Harding, May 25, 1855, MS.

Meanwhile the Legislature had convened and the Senatorial question came on for solution. The history of this contest is generally understood, and the world has repeatedly been told how Lincoln was led to expect the place and would have won but for the apostasy of the five anti-Nebraska men of Democratic antecedents who clung to and finally forced the election of Lyman Trumbull. The student of history in after years will be taught to rever the name of Lincoln for his exceeding magnanimity in inducting his friends to abandon him at the critical period and save Trumbull, while he himself disappeared beneath the waves of defeat.*

This frustration of Lincoln's ambition had a

---

* "After a number of ballots—Judd of Cook, Cook of La Salle, Palmer of Macoupin, and Allen and Baker of Madison voting for Trumbull—I asked Mr. Lincoln what he would advise us to do. He answered, 'Go for Trumbull by all means.' We understood the case to be that Shields was to be run by the Democrats at first and then to be dropped, and Joel A. Matteson put up; and it was calculated that certain of our men who had been elected on the 'Free Soil' issue would vote for him after they had acted with us long enough to satisfy their consciences and constituents. Our object was to force an election before they got through with their programme. We were savagely opposed to Matteson, and so was Mr. Lincoln, who said that if we did not drop in and unite upon Trumbull the five men abovenamed would go for Matteson and elect him, which would be an everlasting disgrace to the State. We reluctantly complied; went to Trumbull and elected him. I remember that Judge S. T. Logan gave up Lincoln with great reluctance. He begged hard to try him on one or two ballots more, but Mr. Lincoln urged us not to risk it longer. I never saw the latter more earnest and decided. He congratulated Trumbull warmly, although of course greatly disappointed and mortified at his own want of success."—Joseph Gillespie, letter, September 19, 1866, MS.

marked effect on his political views. It was plain
to him now that the "irrepressible conflict" was
not far ahead. With the strengthening of his faith
in a just cause so long held in abeyance he became
more defiant each day. But in the very nature of
things he dared not be as bold and outspoken as I.
With him every word and sentence had to be
weighed and its effects calculated, before being
uttered: but with me that operation had to be
reversed if done at all. An incident that occurred
about this time will show how his views were broad-
ening. Some time after the election of Trumbull a
young negro, the son of a colored woman in Springfield known as Polly, went from his home to St.
Louis and there hired as a hand on a lower Mississippi boat,—for what special service, I do not recollect,—arriving in New Orleans without what were
known as free papers. Though born free he was
subjected to the tyranny of the "black code," all
the more stringent because of the recent utterances
of the Abolitionists in the North, and was kept in
prison until his boat had left. Then, as no one was
especially interested in him, he was forgotten. After
a certain length of time established by law, he would
inevitably have been sold into slavery to defray prison
expenses had not Lincoln and I interposed our aid.
The mother came to us with the story of the wrong
done her son and induced us to interfere in her behalf. We went first to see the Governor of Illinois,
who, after patient and thorough examination of the
law, responded that he had no right or power to
interfere. Recourse was then had to the Governor

of Louisiana, who responded in like manner. We were sorely perplexed. A second interview with the Governor of Illinois resulting in nothing favorable Lincoln rose from his chair, hat in hand, and exclaimed with some emphasis: "By God, Governor, I'll make the ground in this country too hot for the foot of a slave, whether you have the legal power to secure the release of this boy or not." Having exhausted all legal means to recover the negro we dropped our relation as lawyers to the case. Lincoln drew up a subscription-list, which I circulated, collecting funds enough to purchase the young man's liberty. The money we sent to Col. A. P. Fields, a friend of ours in New Orleans, who applied it as directed, and it restored the prisoner to his overjoyed mother.

The political history of the country, commencing in 1854 and continuing until the outbreak of the Rebellion, furnishes the student a constant succession of stirring and sometimes bloody scenes. No sooner had Lincoln emerged from the Senatorial contest in February, 1855, and absorbed himself in the law, than the outrages on the borders of Missouri and Kansas began to arrest public attention. The stories of raids, election frauds, murders, and other crimes were moving eastward with marked rapidity. These outbursts of frontier lawlessness, led and sanctioned by the avowed pro-slavery element, were not only stirring up the Abolitionists to fever heat, but touching the hearts of humanity in general. In Illinois an association was formed to aid the cause of "Free-Soil" men in Kansas. In the meetings of

these bands the Abolitionists of course took the
most prominent part. At Springfield we were energetic, vigilant, almost revolutionary. We recommended the employment of any means, however
desperate, to promote and defend the cause of freedom. At one of these meetings Lincoln was called
on for a speech. He responded to the request,
counselling moderation and less bitterness in deal-
ing with the situation before us. We were
belligerent in tone, and clearly out of patience
with the Government. Lincoln opposed the notion
of coercive measures with the possibility of resulting
bloodshed, advising us to eschew resort to the bullet.
"You can better succeed," he declared, "with the
ballot. You can peaceably then redeem the Government and preserve the liberties of mankind
through your votes and voice and moral influence.
. . . . Let there be peace. Revolutionize through
the ballot box, and restore the Government once
more to the affections and hearts of men by making
it express, as it was intended to do, the highest spirit
of justice and liberty. Your attempt, if there be
such, to resist the laws of Kansas by force is criminal
and wicked; and all your feeble attempts will be
follies and end in bringing sorrow on your heads and
ruin the cause you would freely die to preserve!"
These judicious words of counsel, while they reduced
somewhat our ardor and our desperation, only placed
before us in their real colors the grave features of
the situation. We raised a neat sum of money,
Lincoln showing his sincerity by joining in the sub-
scription, and forwarded it to our friends in Kansas.

The Whig party, having accomplished its mission in the political world, was now on the eve of a great break-up. Lincoln realized this and, though proverbially slow in his movements, prepared to find a firm footing when the great rush of waters should come and the maddening freshet sweep former landmarks out of sight. Of the strongest significance in this connection is a letter written by him at this juncture to an old friend in Kentucky,* who called to his attention their differences of views on the wrong of slavery. Speaking of his observation of the treatment of the slaves, he says: "I confess I hate to see the poor creatures hunted down and caught and carried back to their unrequited toils; but I bite my lips and keep quiet. In 1841 you and I had rather a tedious low-water trip on a steamboat from Louisville to St. Louis. You may remember, as I well do, that from Louisville to the mouth of the Ohio, there were on board ten or a dozen slaves shackled together with irons. That sight was a continued torment to me; and I see something like it every time I touch the Ohio or any slave border. It is not fair for you to assume that I have no interest in a thing which has, and continually exercises, the power of making me miserable. You ought rather to appreciate how much the great body of the Northern people do crucify their feelings in order to maintain their loyalty to the Constitution and the Union. I do oppose the extension of slavery because my judgment and feel-

* Letter to Joshua F. Speed, August 24, 1855, MS.

ing so prompt me; and I am under no obligations to
the contrary. If for this you and I must differ,
differ we must."

Finding himself drifting about with the disorgan-
ized elements that floated together after the angry
politicial waters had subsided, it became apparent to
Lincoln that if he expected to figure as a leader he
must take a stand himself. Mere hatred of slavery
and opposition to the injustice of the Kansas-Nebraska legislation were not all that were required of
him. He must be a Democrat, Know-Nothing,
Abolitionist, or Republican, or forever float about in
the great political sea without compass, rudder, or
sail. At length he declared himself. Believing the
times were ripe for more advanced movements, in
the spring of 1856 I drew up a paper for the friends
of freedom to sign, calling a county convention in
Springfield to select delegates for the forthcoming
Republican State convention in Bloomington. The
paper was freely circulated and generously signed.
Lincoln was absent at the time and, believing I
knew what his "feeling and judgment" on the vital
questions of the hour were, I took the liberty to
sign his name to the call. The whole was then published in the Springfield *Journal.* No sooner
had it appeared than John T. Stuart, who, with
others, was endeavoring to retard Lincoln in his
advanced movements, rushed into the office and
excitedly asked it "Lincoln had signed the Abo-
lition call in the *Journal?*" I answered in the negative, adding that I had signed his name myself.
To the question, "Did Lincoln authorize you to

sign it?" I returned an emphatic "No." "Then," exclaimed the startled and indignant Stuart, "you have ruined him." But I was by no means alarmed at what others deemed inconsiderate and hasty action. I thought I understood Lincoln thoroughly, but in order to vindicate myself if assailed I immediately sat down, after Stuart had rushed out of the office, and wrote Lincoln, who was then in Tazewell County attending court, a brief account of what I had done and how much stir it was creating in the ranks of his conservative friends. If he approved or disapproved my course I asked him to write or telegraph me at once. In a brief time came his answer: "All right; go ahead. Will meet you—radicals and all." Stuart subsided, and the conservative spirits who hovered around Springfield no longer held control of the political fortunes of Abraham Lincoln.

The Republican party came into existence in Illinois as a party at Bloomington, May 29, 1856. The State convention of all opponents of anti-Nebraska legislation, referred to in a foregoing paragraph, had been set for that day. Judd, Yates, Trumbull, Swett, and Davis were there; so also was Lovejoy, who, like Otis of colonial fame, was a flame of fire. The firm of Lincoln and Herndon was represented by both members in person. The gallant William H. Bissell, who had ridden at the head of the Second Illinois Regiment at the battle of Buena Vista in the Mexican war, was nominated as governor. The convention adopted a platform ringing with strong anti-Nebraska sentiments, and then and

there gave the Republican party its official christ-
ening. The business of the convention being over,
Mr. Lincoln, in response to repeated calls, came
forward and delivered a speech of such earnestness and power that no one who heard it will ever
forget the effect it produced. In referring to this
speech some years ago I used the following rather
graphic language: "I have heard or read all of Mr.
Lincoln's great speeches, and I give it as my
opinion that the Bloomington speech was the
grand effort of this life. Heretofore he had
simply argued the slavery question on grounds
of policy,—the stateman's grounds,—never reaching the question of the radical and the eternal
right. Now he was newly baptized and freshly
born; he had the fervor of a new convert; the
smothered flame broke out; enthusiasm unusual to
him blazed up; his eyes were aglow with an inspiration; he felt justice; his heart was alive to the
right; his sympathies, remarkably deep for him,
burst forth, and he stood before the throne of the
eternal Right.. His speech was full of fire and
energy and force; it was logic; it was pathos; it
was enthusiasm; it was justice, equity, truth, and
right set ablaze by the divine fires of a soul mad-
dened by the wrong; it was hard, heavy, knotty,
gnarly, backed with wrath. I attempted for about
fifteen minutes as was usual with me then to take
notes, but at the end of that time I threw pen and
paper away and lived only in the inspiration of the
hour. If Mr. Lincoln was six feet, four inches high
usually, at Bloomington that day he was seven feet,

and inspired at that. From that day to the day of his death he stood firm in the right. He felt his great cross, had his great idea, nursed it, kept it, taught it to others, in his fidelity bore witness of it to his death, and finally sealed it with his precious blood." The foregoing paragraph, used by me in a lecture in 1866, may to the average reader seem somewhat vivid in description, besides inclining to extravagance in imagery, yet although more than twenty years have passed since it was written I have never seen the need of altering a single sentence. I still adhere to the substantial truthfulness of the scene as described. Unfortunately Lincoln's speech was never written out nor printed, and we are obliged to depend for its reproduction upon personal recollection.

The Bloomington convention and the part Lincoln took in it met no such hearty response in Springfield as we hoped would follow. It fell flat, and in Lincoln's case drove from him many persons who had heretofore been his warm political friends. A few days after our return we announced a meeting at the court-house to ratify the action of the Bloomington convention. After the usual efforts to draw a crowd, however, only three persons had temerity enough to attend. They were Lincoln, the writer, and a courageous man named John Pain. Lincoln, in answer to the "deafening calls" for a speech, responded that the meeting was larger than he *knew* it would be, and that while he knew that he himself and his partner would attend he was not sure anyone else would, and yet another man had been found brave enough to come out. "While all seems dead," he exhorted, "the age itself is not. It liveth as sure as our Maker liveth. Under all this seeming want of life and motion, the world does move nevertheless. Be hopeful, and now let us adjourn and appeal to the people."

Not only in Springfield but everywhere else the founders of the Republican party—the apostles of freedom—went out to battle for the righteousness of their cause. Lincoln, having as usual been named as one of the Presidential electors, canvassed the State, making in all about fifty speeches. He was in demand everywhere. I have before me a package of letters addressed to him, inviting him to speak at almost every county seat in the State. Yates wanted him to go to one section of the State, Washburne to another, and Trumbull still another; while every cross-roads politician and legislative aspirant wanted him "down in our country, where we need your help." Joshua R. Giddings wrote him words of encouragement. "You may start," said the valiant old Abolitionist in a letter from Peoria,* "on the one great issue of restoring Kansas and Nebraska to freedom, or rather of restoring the Missouri Compromise, and in this State no power on earth can withstand you on that issue." The demand for Lincoln was not confined to his own State. Indiana sent for him, Wisconsin, also, while Norman B. Judd and Ebenezer Peck, who were stumping Iowa, sent for him to come there.

* J. R. Giddings, MS. letter, Sept. 19, 1855.

A town committee invited him to come during "our Equestrian Fair on the 9th, 10th, and 11th," evidently anticipating a three days' siege. An enthusiastic officer in a neighboring town urges him: "Come to our place, because in you do our people place more confidence than in any other man. Men who do not read want the story told as you only can tell it. Others may make fine speeches, but it would not be 'Lincoln said so in his speech.'" A jubilant friend in Chicago writes: "Push on the column of freedom. Give the Buck Africans plenty to do in Egypt. The hour of our redemption draweth nigh. We are coming to Springfield with 20,000 majority!" A postmaster, acting under the courage of his convictions, implores him to visit his neighborhood. "The Democrats here," he insists, "are dyed in the wool. Thunder and lightning would not change their political complexion. I am postmaster here," he adds, confidentially, "for which reason I must ask you to keep this private, for if old Frank (President Pierce) were to hear of my support of Fremont I would get my walking papers sure enough." A settlement of Germans in southern Indiana asked to hear him; and the president of a college, in an invitation to address the students under his charge, characterizes him as "one providentially raised up for a time like this, and even should defeat come in the contest, it would be some consolation to remember we had Hector for a leader."

And thus it was everywhere. Lincoln's importance in the conduct of the campaign was apparent to all, and his canvass was characterized by his usual vigor and effectiveness. He was especially noted for his attempt to break down the strength of Fillmore, who was nominated as a third party candidate and was expected to divide the Republican vote. He tried to wean ·away Fillmore's adherents by an adroit and ingenious letter* sent

---

* One of these letters which Lincoln wrote to counteract the Fillmore movement is still in my possession. As it is more or less characteristic I copy it entire:

"SPRINGFIELD, September 8,.1856.

"HARRISON MALTBY, ESQ.

"*Dear Sir:*

"I understand you are a Fillmore man. Let me prove to you that every vote withheld from Frémont and given to Fillmore in this State actually lessens Fillmore's chance of being President.

"Suppose Buchanan gets all the slave States and Pennsylvania and any other one State besides; then he is elected, no matter who gets all the rest. But suppose Fillmore gets the two slave States of Maryland and Kentucky, then Buchanan is not elected; Fillmore goes into the House of Representatives and may be made President by a compromise. But suppose again Fillmore's friends throw away a few thousand votes on him in Indiana and Illinois; it will inevitably give these States to Buchanan, which will more than compensate him for the loss of Maryland and Kentucky; it will elect him, and leave Fillmore no chance in the House of Representatives or out of it.

"This is as plain as adding up the weight of three small hogs. As Mr. Fillmore has no possible chance to carry Illinois for himself it is plainly to his interest to let Frémont take it and thus keep it out of the hands of Buchanan. Be not deceived. Buchanan is the hard horse to beat in this race. Let him **have** Illinois, and nothing can beat him; and he will get Illinois if men persist in throwing away votes upon Mr. Fillmore. Does some one persuade you that Mr. Fillmore can carry Illinois? Nonsense! There are over seventy newspapers in Illinois opposing Buchanan, only three or four of which support Mr. Fillmore, all the rest going for Frémont. Are not these newspapers a fair index of the proportion of the votes? If not, tell me why.

"Again, of these three or four Fillmore newspapers, two at least are supported in part by the Buchanan men, as I understand. Do not they know where the shoe pinches? They know the Fillmore movement helps them, and therefore they help it.

"Do think these things over and then act according to your judgment.   "Yours very truly,

[Confidential.]   "A. LINCOLN."

to those suspected of the latter s support, and marked confidential, in which he strove to show that in clinging to their candidate they were really aiding the election of Buchanan. But the effort proved unavailing, for in spite of all his arguments and appeals a large number of the Fillmore men clung tenaciously to their leader, resulting in Buchanan's election. The vote in Illinois stood, Buchanan 105,344, Fremont 96,180, and Fillmore 37,451. At the same time Bissell was elected governor by a majority of 4,729 over W. A. Richardson, Democrat. After the heat and burden of the day Lincoln returned home, bearing with him more and greater laurels than ever. The signs of the times indicated, and the result of the canvass demonstrated, that he and he alone was powerful enough to meet the redoubtable Little Giant in a greater conflict yet to follow.

CHAPTER XIII.

I SHALL be forced to omit much that happened during the interval between the election of Buchanan and the campaign of 1858, for the reason that it would not only swell this work to undue proportions, but be a mere repetition of what has been better told by other writers. It is proper to note in passing, however, that Mr. Lincoln's reputation as a political speaker was no longer bounded by the border lines of Illinios. It had passed beyond the Wabash, the Ohio, and the Mississippi rivers, and while his pronounced stand on the slavery question had increased the circle of his admirers in the North it provoled a proportionate amount of execration in the South. He could not help the feeling that he was now the leading Republican in his State, and he was therefore more or less jealous of his prerogative. Formidable in debate, plain in speech, without pretence of literary acquirements, he was none the less self-reliant. He already envied the ascendancy and domination Douglas exercised over his followers, and felt keenly the slight given him by others of his own faith whom he conceived were disposed to prevent his attaining the leadership of his party. I remember early in 1858 of his coming into the office one morning and speaking in very dejected terms of the treatment he was receiving at the hands of Horace Greeley. "I think Greeley," he complained, "is not doing me right. His conduct, I believe, savors a little of injustice. I am a true Republican and have been tried already in the hottest part of the anti-slavery fight, and yet I find him taking up Douglas, a veritable dodger,—once a tool of the South, now its enemy,—and pushing him to the front. He forgets that when he does that he pulls me down at the same time. I fear Greeley's attitude will damage me with Sumner, Seward, Wilson, Phillips, and other friends in the East." This was said with so much of mingled sadness and earnestness that I was deeply impressed. Lincoln was gloomy and restless the entire day. Greeley's letters were driving the enthusiasm out of him.* He seemed unwilling to attend to any business, and finally, just before noon, left the office, going over to the United States Court room to play a game of chess with Judge Treat, and did not return again

---

* Greeley's letters were very pointed and sometimes savage. Here is one:

"I have not proposed to instruct the Republicans of Illinois in their political duties, and I doubt very much that even so much as is implied in your letter can be fairly deduced from anything I have written. Now let me make one prediction. If you run a candidate [for Congress] against Harris and he is able to canvass *he will beat you badly.* He is more of a man at heart and morally than Douglas, and has gone into this fight with more earnestness and less calculation. Of the whole Douglas party he is the truest and best. I never spoke a dozen words with him in my life, having met him but once, but if I lived in his district I should vote for him. As I have never spoken of him in my paper, and suppose I never shall, I take the liberty to say this much to you. Now paddle your own dug-out!

"Yours,
"HORACE GREELEY."

that day. I pondered a good deal over Lincoln's dejection, and that night, after weighing the matter well in mind, resolved to go to the eastern States myself and endeavor to sound some of the great men there. The next day, on apprising Lincoln of my determination, he questioned its propriety. Our relations, he insisted, were so intimate that a wrong construction might be put upon the movement. I listened carefully to him, but as I had never been beyond the Alleghanies I packed my valise and went, notwithstanding his objections. I had been in correspondence on my own account with Greeley, Seward, Sumner, Phillips, and others for several years, had kept them informed of the feelings of our people and the political campaigns in their various stages, but had never met any of them save Greeley. I enjoyed heartily the journey and the varied sights and scenes that attended it. Aside from my mission, the trip was a great success. The magnificent buildings, the display of wealth in the large cities and prosperous manufacturing towns, broadened the views of one whose vision had never extended beyond the limits of the Illinois prairies. In Washington I saw and dined with Trumbull, who went over the situation with me. Trumbull had written to Lincoln shortly before* that he thought it "useless to speculate upon the further course of Douglas or the effect it is to have in Illinois or other States. He himself does not know where he is going or where he will come out." At my interview with Trumbull, however, he directed me to

---

* Letter, December 25, 1857, MS.

assure Mr. Lincoln that Douglas did not mean to join the Republican party, however great the breach between himself and the administration might be. "We Republicans here," he said exultingly in another letter to Lincoln, "are in good spirits, and are standing back to let the fight go on between Douglas and his former associates. Lincoln will lose nothing by this if he can keep the attention of our Illinois people from being diverted from the great and vital question of the day to the minor and temporary issues which are now being discussed."* In Washington I saw also Seward, Wilson, and others of equal prominence. Douglas was confined to his house by illness, but on receiving my card he directed me to be shown up to his room. We had a pleasant and interesting interview. Of course the conversation soon turned on Lincoln. In answer to an inquiry regarding the latter I remarked that Lincoln was pursuing the even tenor of his way. "He is not in anybody's way," I contended, "not even in yours, Judge Douglas." He was sitting up in a chair smoking a cigar. Between puffs he responded that neither was he in the way of Lincoln or any one else, and did not intend to invite conflict. He conceived that he had achieved what he had set out to do, and hence did not feel that his course need put him in opposition to Mr. Lincoln or his party. "Give Mr. Lincoln my regards," he said, rather warmly, "when you return, and tell him I have crossed the river and

---

* Letter, December 27, 1857, MS.

burned my boat." Leaving Washington, my next
point was New York, where I met the editor of the
Anti-Slavery Standard, Horace Greeley, Henry
Ward Beecher, and others. I had a long talk with
Geeley, whom I noticed leaned toward Douglas. I
found, however, he was not at all hostile to Lincoln.
I presented the latter's case in the best phase I knew
how, but while I drew but little from him, I left
feeling that he hadn't been entirely won over. He
introduced me to Beecher, who, as everybody else
did, inquired after Lincoln and through me sent
him words of encouragement and praise.* From
New York I went to Boston, and from the latter place
I wrote Lincoln a letter which happily I found not
long since in a bundle of Lincoln's letters, and
which I insert here, believing it affords a better
reflex of the situation at the time than anything I
might see fit to say now. Here it is:

"REVERE HOUSE,
"BOSTON, MASS., March 24, 1858.
"FRIEND LINCOLN.

"I am in this city of notions, and am well—very
well indeed. I wrote you a hasty letter from
Washington some days ago, since which time I
have been in Philadelphia, Baltimore, New York,
and now here. I saw Greeley, and so far as any of
our conversation is interesting to you I will relate.
And we talked, say twenty minutes. He evidently

---

* Lincoln's greatest fear was that Douglas might be taken up
by the Republicans. Senator Seward, when I met him in Washington, assured me there was no danger of it, insisting that the
Republicans nor any one else could place any reliance on a man
so slippery as Douglas.

wants Douglas sustained and sent back to the Senate. He did not say so in so many words, yet his *feelings* are with Douglas. I *know* it from the spirit and drift of his conversation. He talked bitterly—somewhat so—against the papers in Illinois, and said they were fools. I asked him this question, 'Greeley, do you want to see a third party organized, or do you want Douglas to ride to power through the North, which he has so much abused and betrayed?' and to which he replied, 'Let the future alone; it will all come right. Douglas is a brave man. Forget the past and sustain the *righteous.*' Good God, *righteous,* eh!

"Since I have landed in Boston I have seen much that was entertaining and interesting. This morning I was introduced to Governor Banks. He and I had a conversation about Republicanism and especially about Douglas. He asked me this question, 'You will sustain Douglas in Illinois, wont you?' and to which I said '*No, never!*' He affected to be much surprised, and so the matter dropped and turned on Republicanism, or in general—Lincoln. Greeley's and other sheets that laud Douglas, Harris, *et al.*, want them sustained, and will *try* to do it. Several persons have asked me the same question which Banks asked, and evidently they get their cue, ideas, or what not from Greeley, Seward, *et al.* By-the-bye, Greeley remarked· to me this, 'The Republican standard is too high; we want something practical.'

"This may not be interesting to you, but, however it may be, it is my duty to state what is going on, so that you may head it off—counteract it in some way. I hope it can be done. The northern men are cold to me—somewhat repellent.

"Your friend,

"W. H. HERNDON."

On my return home I had encouraging news to relate. I told Lincoln of the favorable mention I had heard of him by Phillips, Sumner, Seward, Garrison, Beecher, and Greeley. I brought with me additional sermons and lectures by Theodore Parker, who was warm in his commendation of Lincoln. One of these was a lecture on "The Effect of Slavery on the American People," which was delivered in the Music Hall in Boston, and which I gave to Lincoln, who read and returned it. He liked especially the following expression, which he marked with a pencil, and which he in substance afterwards used in his Gettysburg address: "Democracy is direct self-government, over all the people, for all the people, by all the people."

Meanwhile, passing by other events which have become interwoven in the history of the land, we reach April, 1858, at which time the Democratic State convention met and, besides nominating candidates for State offices, endorsed Mr. Douglas' services in the Senate, thereby virtually renominating him for that exalted office. In the very nature of things Lincoln was the man already chosen in the hearts of the Republicans of Illinois for the same office, and therefore with singular appropriateness they passed, with great unanimity, at their convention in Springfield on the 16th of June, the characteristic resolution: "That Hon. Abraham Lincoln is our first and only choice for United States Senator to fill the vacancy about to be created by the expiration of Mr. Douglas' term of office." There was of course no surprise in this for Mr. Lincoln. He had been all along led to expect it, and with that in view had been earnestly and quietly at work preparing a speech in acknowledgment of the honor about to be conferred on him. This speech he wrote on stray envelopes and scraps of paper, as ideas suggested themselves, putting them into that miscellaneous and convenient receptacle, his hat. As the convention drew near he copied the whole on connected sheets, carefully revising every line and sentence, and fastened them together, for reference during the delivery of the speech, and for publication. The former precaution, however, was unnecessary, for he had studied and read over what he had written so long and carefully that he was able to deliver it without the least hesitation or difficulty. A few days before the convention, when he was at work on the speech, I remember that Jesse K. Dubois,* who was Auditor of State, came into the office and, seeing Lincoln busily writing, inquired what he was doing or what he was writing. Lincoln answered gruffly, "It's something you may see or hear sometime, but I'll not let you see it now." I myself knew what he was writing, but having asked neither my opinion nor that of anyone else, I did not venture to

---

* "After the covention Lincoln met me on the street and said, 'Dubois, I can tell you now what I was doing the other day when you came into my office. I was writing that speech, and I knew if I read the passage about the "house divided against itself" to you, you would ask me to change or modify it, and that I was determined not to do. I had willed it so, and was willing if necessary to perish with it."—Statement of Jesse K. Dubois, MS.

offer any suggestions. After he had finished the
final draft of the speech, he locked the office door,
drew the curtain across the glass panel in the door,
and read it to me. At the end of each paragraph
he would halt and wait for my comments. I remember what I said after hearing the first paragraph, wherein occurs the celebrated figure of the
house divided against itself: "It is true, but is it
wise or politic to say so?" He responded: "That
expression is a truth of all human experience, 'a
house divided against itself cannot stand,' and 'he
that runs may read.' The proposition also is true,
and has been for six thousand years. I want to
use some universally known figure expressed in
simple language as universally well-known, that
may strike home to the minds of men in order to
raise them up to the peril of the times. I do not
believe I would be right in changing or omitting it.
I would rather be defeated with this expression in
the speech, and uphold and discuss it before the
people, than be victorious without it." This was
not the first time Lincoln had endorsed the dogma
that our Government could not long endure part
slave and part free. He had incorporated it in a
speech at Bloomington in 1856, but in obedience to
the emphatic protest of Judge T. Lyle Dickey and
others, who conceived the idea that its "delivery
would make Abolitionists of all the North and
slavery propagandists of all the South, and thereby
precipitate a struggle which might end in dis-
union," he consented to suspend its repitition, but

only for that campaign.* Now, however, the situation had changed somewhat. There had been a shifting of scenes, so to speak. The Republican party had gained some in strength and more in moral effectiveness and force. Nothing could keep back in Lincoln any longer, sentiments of right and truth, and he prepared to give the fullest expression to both in all future contests.

Before delivering his speech he invited a dozen or so of his friends over to the library of the State House, where he read and submitted it to them. After the reading he asked each man for his opinion. Some condemned and not one endorsed it. One man, more forcible than elegant, characterized it as a "d—d fool utterance;" another said the doctrine was "ahead of its time;" and still another contended that it would drive away a good many voters fresh from the Democrats ranks. Each man attacked it in his criticism. I was the last to respond. Although the doctrine announced was

---

* "After the meeting was over Mr. Lincoln and I returned to the Pike House, where we occupied the same room. Immediately on reaching the room I said to him, 'What in God's name could induce you to promulgate such an opinion?' He replied familiarly, 'Upon my soul, Dickey, I think it is true.' I reasoned to show it was not a correct opinion. He argued strenuously that the opinion was a sound one. At length I said, 'Suppose you are right, that our Government cannot last part free and part slave, what good is to be accomplished by inculcating that opinion (or truth, if you please) in the minds of the people?' After some minutes reflection he rose and approached me, extending his right hand to take mine, and said, 'From respect for you judgment, Dickey, I'll promise you I won't teach the doctrine again during this campaign.' "—Letter, T. Lyle Dickey, MS., December 8, 1866.

rather rank, yet it suited my views, and I said,
"Lincoln, deliver that speech as read and it will
make you President." At the time I hardly
realized the force of my prophecy. Having patiently
listened to these various criticisms from his friends
—all of which with a single exception were adverse—he rose from his chair, and after alluding to
the careful study and intense thought he had given
the question, he answered all their objections substantially as follows: "Friends, this thing has been
retarded long enough. The time has come when
these sentiments should be uttered; and if it is
decreed that I should go down because of this
speech, then let me go down linked to the truth—
let me die in the advocacy of what is just and
right." The next day, the 17th, the speech was
delivered just as we had heard it read. Up to this
time Seward had held sway over the North by his
"higher-law" sentiments, but the "house-divided-
against-itself" speech by Lincoln in my opinion
drove the nail into Seward's political coffin.*

Lincoln had now created in reality a more profound impression than he or his friends anticipated.
Many Republicans deprecated the advanced ground
he had taken, the more so as the Democrats re-
joiced that it afforded them an issue clear and

* In any student of oratorical history, after reading Lincoln's
speech on this occasion, will refer to Webster's reply to Hayne
in the Senate, he will be struck with the similarity in figure and
thought in the opening lines of both speeches. In fact, it may
not be amiss to note that, in this instance, Webster's effort was
carefully read by Lincoln and served in part as his model.

well-defined. Numbers of his friends distant from Springfield, on reading his speech, wrote him censorious letters; and one well-informed co-worker* predicted his defeat, charging it to the first ten lines of the speech. These complaints, coming apparently from every quarter, Lincoln bore with great patience. To one complainant who followed him into his office he said proudly. "If I had to draw a pen across my record, and erase my whole life from sight, and I had one poor gift or choice left as to what I should save from the wreck, I should choose that speech and leave it to the world unerased."

Meanwhile Douglas had returned from Washington to his home in Chicago. Here he rested for a few days until his friends and co-workers had arranged the details of a public reception on the 9th of July, when he delivered from the balcony of the Tremont House a speech intended as an answer to the one made by Lincoln in Springfield. Lincoln was present at this reception, but took no part in it. The next day, however, he replied. Both speeches were delivered at the same place. Leaving Chicago, Douglas passed on down to Bloomington and Springfield, where he spoke on the 16th and 17th of July respectively. On the evening of the latter day Lincoln responded again in a most effective and convincing effort. The contest now took on a different phase. Lincoln's Republican friends urged him to draw Douglas into a joint debate, and he accordingly sent him a challenge on the 24th of

---

* Leonard Swett.

July. It is not necessary, I suppose, to reproduce here the correspondence that passed between these great leaders. On the 30th Douglas finally accepted the proposition to "divide time, and address the same audiences," naming seven different places, one in each Congressional district, outside of Chicago and Springfield, for joint meetings.* The places and dates were, Ottawa, August 21; Freeport, August 27; Jonesboro, September 15; Charleston, September 18, Galesburg, October 7; Quincy,

---

* Among the items of preparation on Lincoln's part hitherto withheld is the following letter, which explains itself:

"SPRINGFIELD, June 28, 1858.

"A. CAMPBELL, Esq.

"MY DEAR SIR:—In 1856 you gave me authority to draw on you for any sum not exceeding five hundred dollars. I see clearly that such a privilege would be more available now than it was then. I am aware that times are tighter now than they were then. Please write me at all events, and whether you can now do anything or not I shall continue grateful for the past.

"Yours very truly,
"A. LINCOLN."

* The following recent letter from Mr. Campbell is not without interest:

LA SALLE, ILL., Dec. 12th, 1888.

"JESSE W. WEIK, Esq.

"MY DEAR SIR:—I gave Mr. Lincoln some money in the office of Lincoln & Herndon in Springfield in 1856, but I do not remember the exact amount. It was, however, between two and three hundred dollars. I never had Mr. Lincoln's obligation for the payment of any money. I never kept any account of nor charged my memory with any money I gave him. It was given to defray his personal expenses and otherwise promote the interest of a cause which I sincerely believed to be for the public good, and without the thought or expectation of a dollar of it ever being returned. From what I knew and learned of his careful habits in money matters in the campaign of 1856 I am entirely confident that every dollar and dime I ever gave was carefully and faithfully applied to the uses and purposes for which it was given.

"Sincerely yours,
"A. CAMPBELL."

October 13; and Alton, October 15. "I agree
to your suggestion," wrote Douglas, "that we shall
alternately open and close the discussion. I will
speak at Ottawa one hour, you can reply, occupying
an hour and a half, and I will then follow for half
an hour. At Freeport you shall open the discussion and speak one hour, I will follow for an hour
and a half, and you can then reply for half an hour.
We will alternate in like manner in each successive
place." To this arrangement Lincoln on the 31st
gave his consent, "although," he wrote, "by the
terms as you propose you take four openings and
closes to my three."

History furnishes few characters whose lives and
careers were so nearly parallel as those of Lincoln
and Douglas. They met for the first time at the
Legislature in Vandalia in 1834, where Lincoln was
a member of the House of Representatives and
Douglas was in the lobby. The next year Douglas
was also a member. In 1839 both were admitted to
practice in the Supreme Court of Illinois on the
same day.* In 1841 both courted the same young
lady. In 1846 both represented Illinois in Congress
at Washington, the one in the upper and the other
in the lower House. In 1858 they were opposing
candidates for United States Senator; and finally, to
complete the remarkable counterpart, both were
candidates for the Presidency in 1860. While it is
true that their ambitions ran in parallel lines, yet
they were exceedingly unlike in all other particulars.

* December 3d.

Douglas was short,—something over five feet high,—
heavy set, with a large head, broad shoulders, deep
chest, and striking features. He was polite and
affable, but fearless. He had that unique trait,
magnetism, fully developed in his nature, and that
attracted a host of friends and readily made him a
popular idol. He had had extensive experience in
debate, and had been trained by contact for years
with the great minds and orators in Congress.
He was full of political history, well informed
on general topics, eloquent almost to the point
of brilliancy, self-confident to the point of arrogance,
and a dangerous competitor in every respect. What
he lacked in ingenuity he made up in strategy, and
if in debate he could not tear down the struct-
ure of this opponent's argument by a direct and
violent attack, he was by no means reluctant to
resort to a strained restatement of the latter's position or to the extravagance of ridicule. Lincoln
knew his man thoroughly and well.* He had
often met Douglas on the stump; was familiar with
his tactics, and though fully aware of his "want of

---

* An erroneous impression has grown up in recent years concerning Douglas's ability and standing as a lawyer. One of the
latest biographies of Lincoln credits him with many of the arti-
fices of the "shyster." This is not only unfair, but decidedly untrue. I always found Douglas at the bar to be a broad, fair,
and liberal-minded man. Although not a thorough student of
the law his large fund of good common-sense kept him in the
front rank. He was equally generous and courteous, and he
never stooped to gain a case. I know that Lincoln entertained
the same view of him. It was only in politics that Douglas
demonstrated any want of inflexibility and rectitude, and then
only did Lincoln manifest a lack of faith in his morals.

fixed political morals," was not averse to measuring swords with the elastic and flexible "Little Giant."

Lincoln himself was constructed on an entirely different foundation. His base was plain common-sense, direct statement, and the inflexibility of logic. In physical make-up he was cold—at least not magnetic—and made no effort to dazzle people by his bearing. He cared nothing for a following, and though he had often before struggled for a polit-ical prize, yet in his efforts he never had strained his well-known spirit of fairness or open love of the truth. He analyzed everything, laid every state-ment bare, and by dint of his broad reasoning pow-ers and manliness of admission inspired his hearers with deep conviction of his earnestness and hon-esty. Douglas may have electrified the crowds with his eloquence or charmed them with his majestic bearing and dexterity in debate, but as each man, after the meetings were over and the applause had died away, went to his home, his head rang with Lincoln's logic and appeal to manhood.

A brief description of Mr. Lincoln's appearance on the stump and of his manner when speaking may not be without interest. When standing erect he was six feet four inches high. He was lean in flesh and ungainly in figure. Aside from the sad, pained look due to habitual melancholy, his face had no characteristic or fixed expression. He was thin through the chest, and hence slightly stoop-shoul-dered. When he arose to address courts, juries, or crowds of people, his body inclined forward to a

slight degree. At first he was very awkward, and it
seemed a real labor to adjust himself to his surroundings. He struggled for a time under a feeling of apparent diffidence and sensitiveness, and
these only added to his awkwardness. I have often
seen and sympathized with Mr. Lincoln during
these moments. When he began speaking, his
voice was shrill, piping, and unpleasant. His manner, his attitude, his dark, yellow face, wrinkled and
dry, his oddity of pose, his diffident movements—
everything seemed to be against him, but only for
a short time. After having arisen, he generally
placed his hands behind him, the back of his left
hand in the palm of his right, the thumb and
fingers of his right hand clasped around the left
arm at the wrist. For a few moments he played
the combination of awkwardness, sensitiveness, and
diffidence. As he proceeded he became somewhat
animated, and to keep in harmony with his growing
warmth his hands relaxed their grasp and fell to
his side. Presently he clasped them in front of
him, interlocking his fingers, one thumb meanwhile
chasing another. His speech now requiring more
emphatic utterance, his fingers unlocked and his
hands fell apart. His left arm was thrown behind,
the back of his hand resting against his body, his
right hand seeking his side. By this time he had
gained sufficient composure, and his real speech
began. He did not gesticulate as much with
his hands as with his head. He used the latter frequently, throwing it with vim this way and that.
This movement was a significant one when he

sought to enforce his statement. It sometimes
came with a quick jerk, as if throwing off electric
sparks into combustible material. He never sawed
the air nor rent space into tatters and rags as some
orators do. He never acted for stage effect. He
was cool, considerate, reflective—in time self-pos-
sessed and self-reliant. His style was clear, terse,
and compact. In argument he was logical, demon-
strative, and fair. He was careless of his dress, and
his clothes, instead of fitting neatly as did the gar-
ments of Douglas on the latter's well-rounded form,
hung loosely on his giant frame. As he moved
along in his speech he became freer and less uneasy
in his movements; to that extent he was graceful.
He had a perfect naturalness, a strong individuality; and to that extent he was dignified. He
despised glitter, show, set forms, and shams. He
spoke with effectiveness and to move the judgment as well as the emotions of men. There was
a world of meaning and emphasis in the long, bony
finger of his right hand as he dotted the ideas on
the minds of his hearers. Sometimes, to express
joy or pleasure, he would raise both hands at an
angle of about fifty degrees, the palms upwards, as
if desirous of embracing the spirit of that which he
loved. If the sentiment was one of detestation—
denunciation of slavery, for example—both arms,
thrown upward and fists clenched, swept through the
air, and he expressed an execration that was truly
sublime. This was one of his most effective gestures,
and signified most vividly a fixed determination to
drag down the object of his hatred and trample it

in the dust. He always stood squarely on his feet, toe even with toe; that is, he never put one foot before the other. He neither touched nor leaned on anything for support. He made but few changes in his positions and attitudes. He never ranted, never walked backward and forward on the platform. To ease his arms he frequently caught hold, with his left hand, of the lapel of his coat, keeping his thumb upright and leaving his right hand free to gesticulate. The designer of the monument recently erected in Chicago has happily caught him in just this attitude. As he proceeded with his speech the exercise of his vocal organs altered somewhat the tone of his voice. It lost in a measure its former acute and shrilling pitch, and mellowed into a more harmonious and pleasant sound. His form expanded, and, notwithstanding the sunken breast, he rose up a splendid and imposing figure. In his defence of the Declaration of Independence—his greatest inspiration—he was "tremendous in the directness of his utterances; he rose to impassioned eloquence, unsurpassed by Patrick Henry, Mirabeau, or Vergniaud, as his soul was inspired with the thought of human right and Divine justice."* His little gray eyes flashed in a face aglow with the fire of his profound thoughts; and his uneasy movements and diffident manner sunk themselves beneath the wave of righteous indignation that came sweeping over him. Such was Lincoln the orator.

---

* Horace White, who was present and reported the speech for his paper, the Chicago *Tribune*. Letter, June 9, 1865, MS.

We can somewhat appreciate the feeling with which Douglas, aggressive and fearless though he was, welcomed a contest with such a man as Lincoln. Four years before, in a joint debate with him, he had asked for a cessation of forensic hostilities, conceding that his opponent of rail-splitting fame had given him "more trouble than all the United States Senate together." Now he was brought face to face with him again.*

It is unnecessary and not in keeping with the purpose of this work to reproduce here the speeches made by either Lincoln or Douglas in their justly renowned debate. Briefly stated, Lincoln's position was announced in his opening speech at Springfield: " 'A house divided against itself cannot stand.' I believe this Government cannot endure permanently half slave and half free. I do not expect the Union to be dissolved, I do not expect the house to fall—but I do expect it will cease to be divided. It will become all the one thing or the other. Either the opponents of slavery will arrest the further spread of it and place it where the public mind shall rest in the belief that it is in the course of ultimate extinction; or its advocates will push it forward till it becomes alike lawful in all the states, old as well as new, North as well as South." The position of Douglas on the question of slavery was one of indifference. He advocated

---

* "Douglas and I, for the first time this canvass, crossed swords here yesterday. The fire flew some, and I am glad to know I am yet alive."—Lincoln to J. O. Cunningham, Ottawa, Ul. August 22 1858, MS.

with all his power the doctrine of "Popular Sovereignty," a proposition, as quaintly put by Lincoln, which meant that, "if one man chooses to enslave another, no third man has a right to object." At the last joint discussion in Alton, Lincoln, after reflecting on the patriotism of any man who was so indifferent to the wrong of slavery that he cared not whether it was voted up or down, closed his speech with this stirring summary: "That [slavery] is the real issue. That is the issue that will continue in this country when these poor tongues of Judge Douglas and myself shall be silent. It is the eternal struggle between these two principles —right and wrong—throughout the world. They are the two principles that have stood face to face from the beginning of time, and will ever continue to struggle. The one is the common right of humanity, and the other the divine right of kings. It is the same principle, in whatever shape it developes itself. It is the same spirit that says: 'You work and toil and earn bread, and I eat it.' No matter in what shape it comes, whether from the mouth of a king who seeks to bestride the people of his own nation and live by the fruit of their labor, or from one race of men as an apology for enslaving another race, it is the same tyrannical principle."

It is unnecessary, I presume, to insert here the seven questions which Douglas propounded to Lincoln at their first meeting at Ottawa, nor the historic four which Lincoln asked at Freeport. It only remains to say that in answering Lincoln at

Freeport, Douglas accomplished his own political downfall. He was swept entirely away from his former foundation, and even the glory of a subsequent election to the Senate never restored him to it.

During the canvass Mr. Lincoln, in addition to the seven meetings with Douglas, filled thirty-one appointments made by the State Central Committee, besides speaking at many other times and places not previously advertised. In his trips to and fro over the State, between meetings, he would stop at Springfield sometimes, to consult with his friends or to post himself up on questions that occurred during the canvass. He kept me busy hunting up old speeches and gathering facts and statistics at the State library. I made liberal clippings bearing in any way on the questions of the hour from every newspaper I happened to see, and kept him supplied with them; and on one or two occasions, in answer to letters and telegrams, I sent books forward to him. He had a little leather bound book, fastened in front with a clasp, in which he and I both kept inserting newspaper slips and newspaper comments until the canvass opened. In arranging for the joint meetings and managing the crowds Douglas enjoyed one great advantage. He had been United States Senator for several years, and had influential friends holding comfortable government offices all over the State. These men were on hand at every meeting, losing no opportunity to applaud lustily all the points Douglas made and to lionize him in every conceivable way. The ingeniously contrived display of their enthusiasm had a marked effect on certain crowds—a fact of which Lincoln frequently complained to his friends. One who accompanied him during the canvass* relates this: "Lincoln and I were at the Centralia agricultural fair the day after the debate at Jonesboro. Night came on and we were tired, having been on the fair grounds all day. We were to go north on the Illinois Central railroad. The train was due at midnight, and the depot was full of people. I managed to get a chair for Lincoln in the office of the superintendent of the railroad, but small politicians would intrude so that he could scarcely get a moment's sleep. The train came and was filled instantly. I got a seat near the door for Lincoln and myself. He was worn out, and had to meet Douglas the next day at Charleston. An empty car, called a saloon car, was hitched on to the rear of the train and locked up. I asked the conductor, who knew Lincoln and myself well,—we were both attorneys of the road,—if Lincoln could not ride in that car; that he was exhausted and needed rest; but the conductor refused. I afterwards got him in by a stratagem. At the same time George B. McClellan in person was taking Douglas around in a special car and special train; and that was the unjust treatment Lincoln got from the Illinois Central railroad. Every interest of that road and every employee was against Lincoln and for Douglas."

The heat and dust and bonfires of the campaign

* Henry C. Whitney, MS., July 21, 1865.

at last came to an end. The election took place on
the second of November, and while Lincoln received
of the popular vote a majority of over four thousand, yet the returns from the legislative districts
foreshadowed his defeat. In fact, when the Senatorial election took place in the Legislature,
Douglas received fifty four and Lincoln forty-six
votes—one of the results of the lamentable appor-
tionment law then in operation.*

The letters of Lincoln at this period are the best
evidence of his feelings now obtainable, and of how
he accepted his defeat. To Henry Asbury, a
friend who had written him a cheerful letter ad-

---

* Horace Greeley was one of the most vigilant men during the
debate. He wrote to Lincoln and me many letters which I
still retain. In a letter to me during the campaign, October 6,
he says with reference to Douglas: "In his present position I
could not of course support him, but he need not have been in
this position had the Republicans of Illinois been as wise and
far-seeing as they are earnest and true. . . . but seeing things
are as they are, I do not wish to be quoted as authority for
making trouble and division among our friends." Soon after
hearing of the result of November election he again writes:
"I advise you privately that Mr. Douglas would be the strongest candidate that the Democratic party could present for President; but they will not present him. The old leaders wouldn't
endorse it. As he is doomed to be slaughtered at Charleston
it is good policy to fatten him meantime. He will cut up the
better at killing time." An inquiry for his preference as to
Presidential timber elicited this response, December 4th. "As
to President, my present judgment is Edward Bates, with John
M. Read for Vice; but I am willing to go anything that looks
strong I don't wish to load the team heavier than it will pull
through. As to Douglas, he is like the man's boy who (he said)
'didn't weigh so much as he expected, and he always knew he
wouldn't.' I never thought him very sound coin; but I didn't
think it best to beat him on the back of his anti-Lecompton
fight, and I am still of that opinion."

monishing him not to give up the battle, he responded:

"SPRINGFIELD, November 19, 1858.

"MR. HENRY ASBURY,

"*My Dear Sir:*—Yours of the 13th was received some days ago. The fight must go on. The cause of civil liberty must not be surrendered at the end of one or even one hundred defeats. Douglas had the ingenuity to be supported in the late contest both as the best means to break down and to uphold the slave interest. No ingenuity can keep these antagonistic elements in harmony long. Another explosion will soon come.

"Yours truly,
"A. LINCOLN.'

To another friend* on the same day he writes: "I am glad I made the late race. It gave me a hearing on the great and durable questions of the age which I could have had in no other way; and though I now sink out of view and shall be forgotten, I believe I have made some marks which will tell for the cause of liberty long after I am gone."

Before passing to later events in Mr. Lincoln's life it is proper to include in this chapter, as a specimen of his oratory at this time, his eloquent reference to the Declaration of Independence found in a speech delivered at Beardstown, August 12, and not at Lewiston five days later, as many biographers have it. Aside from its concise reasoning, the sublime thought it suggests entitles it to rank beside that great masterpiece, his Gettysburg

---

* Dr. Henry.

address. After alluding to the suppression by the
Fathers of the Republic of the slave trade, he says:
"These by their representatives in old Independence Hall said to the whole race of men: 'We
hold these truths to be self-evident: that all men
are created equal; that they are endowed by their
Creator with certain inalienable rights; that among
these are life, liberty, and the pursuit of happiness.'
This was their majestic interpretation of the econ-
omy of the universe. This was their lofty, and
wise, and noble understanding of the justice of the
Creator to his creatures—yes, gentlemen, to all his
creatures, to the whole great family of man. In
their enlightened belief, nothing stamped with the
divine image and likeness was sent into the world
to be trodden on and degraded and imbruted by
its fellows. They grasped not only the whole race
of man then living, but they reached forward and
seized upon the farthest posterity. They erected
a beacon to guide their children, and their children's
children, and the countless myriads who should in-
habit the earth in other ages. Wise statesmen as
they were, they knew the tendency of prosperity to
breed tyrants, and so they established these great
self-evident truths, that when in the distant future
some man, some faction, some interest, should set
up the doctrine that none but rich men, none but
white men, or none but Anglo-Saxon white men
were entitled to life, liberty, and the pursuit of happiness, their posterity might look up again to the
Declaration of Independence and take courage
to renew the battle which their fathers began,

so that truth and justice and mercy and all the humane and Christian virtues might not be extinguished from the land; so that no man would hereafter dare to limit and circumscribe the great principles on which the temple of liberty was being built.

"Now, my countrymen, if you have been taught doctrines conflicting with the great landmarks of the Declaration of Independence; if you have listened to suggestions which would take away from its grandeur and mutilate the fair symmetry of its proportions; if you have been inclined to believe that all men are not created equal in those inalienable rights enumerated by our chart of liberty: let me entreat you to come back. Return to the fountain whose waters spring close by the blood of the Revolution. Think nothing of me; take no thought for the political fate of any man whomsoever, but come back to the truths that are in the Declaration of Independence. You may do anything with me you choose, if you will but heed these sacred principles. You may not only defeat me for the Senate, but you may take me and put me to death. While pretending no indifference to earthly honors, I do claim to be actuated in this contest by something higher than an anxiety for office. I charge you to drop every paltry and insignificant thought for any man's success. It is nothing; I am nothing; Judge Douglas is nothing. But do not destroy that immortal emblem of humanity—the Declaration of American Independence."

One of the newspaper men* who heard this majestic oration wrote me as follows: "The apostrophe to the Declaration of Independence to which you refer was written by myself from a vivid recollection of Mr. Lincoln's speech at Beardstown, August 12, 1858. On the day following the delivery of the speech, as Mr. Lincoln and I were proceeding by steamer from Beardstown to Havana, I said to him that I had been greatly impressed by his concluding remarks of the day previous, and that if he would write them out for me I felt confident their publication would be highly beneficial to our cause as well as honorable to his own fame. He replied that he had but a faint recollection of any portion of the speech; that, like all his campaign speeches, it was necessarily extemporaneous; and that its good or bad effect depended upon the inspiration of the moment. He added that I had probably over-estimated the value of the remarks referred to. In reply to my question whether he had any objection to my writing them out from memory and putting them in the form of a verbatim report, he said, 'None at all.' I accordingly did so. I felt confident then and I feel equally assured now that I transcribed the peroration with absolute fidelity as to ideas and commendable fidelity as to language. I certainly aimed to reproduce his exact words, and my recollection of the passage as spoken was very clear. After I had finished writing I read it to Mr. Lincoln. When I had finished the reading he said,

* Horace White, MS., May 17, 1865.

'Well, those are my views, and if I said anything on
the subject I must have said substantially that, but
not nearly so well as that is said.' I remember
this remark quite distinctly, and if the old steamer
Editor is still in existence I could show the place
where we were sitting. Having secured his assent
to the publication I forwarded it to our paper, but
inasmuch as my report of the Beardstown meeting
had been already mailed I incorporated the remarks
on the Declaration of Independence in my letter
from Lewiston two or three days subsequently.
. . . . I do not remember ever having related
these facts before, although they have often recurred
to me as I have seen the peroration resuscitated
again and again, and published (with good effect, I
trust) in the newspapers of this country and England."

Printed in the United States
134487LV00007B/126/A